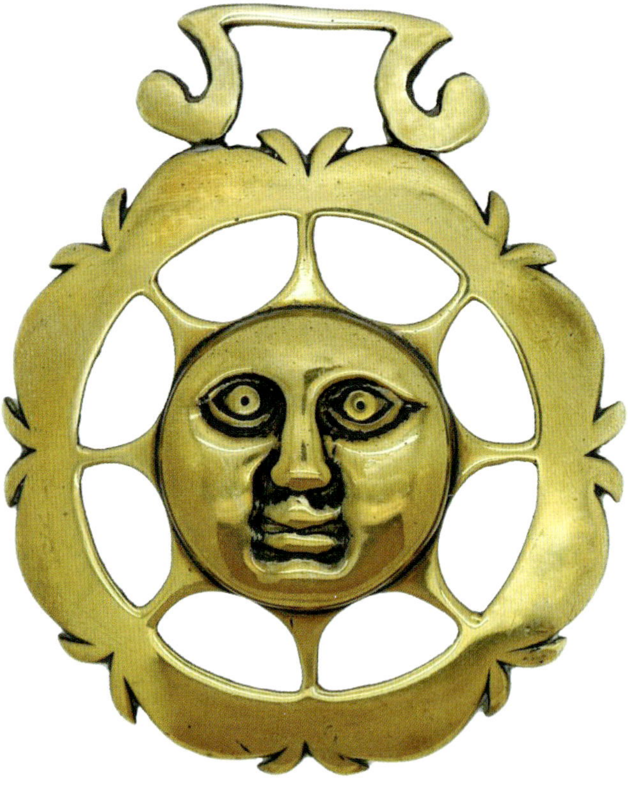

# The Collector's Anthology of Antique Horse Brasses

VOLUME II

May Day turnout c.1905 in the market town of Morely, borough of Leeds, Yorkshire, England

# The Collector's Anthology

## of

# Antique Horse Brasses

✳ ✳ ✳

Richard Bradshaw and Ian Jones

A publication of the National Horse Brass Society
Great Britain

VOLUME II

*Copyright © National Horse Brass Society 2017*

*All rights reserved. No part of this publication may be reproduced, stored in a retrieval system or transmitted, in any form or by any means, electronic, mechanical, photocopying, recording or otherwise, without the prior written permission of the National Horse Brass Society.*

✳✳✳

*First published 2017*
*ISBN 978-0-9931814-9-8*

✳✳✳

*Printed in Great Britain by*
*Northend Creative Print Solutions*
*Clyde Road, Sheffield S8 0TZ*

# Contents

**Foreword** .......................... 7

**Regional Styles**
   Scotland & North East ..... 8
   Merseyside ……………... 13
   West Yorkshire ………… 19
   Wales & Shropshire …….. 20
   West Sussex ……………. 22
   South Yorkshire …………. 24

**Awards** .......................... 28

**Saddlers** ……………….. 35

**Nosebands** …………….. 41

**Martingales** ……………. 45

**Hameplates** …………….. 51

**Commemoratives** ………… 57

**Brewery** …………………. 65

**Trade & Transport** ……….. 71

**Vestry** ………………….. 75

**Owner & Farmer** ………… 79

**War & Peace** ……………. 82

**Noah's Ark** ……………… 85

**Swingers** ……………….. 91

**Patterns & Oddities** …….. 100

**Acknowledgements** ……… 102

We ought to envy collectors,
for they brighten their days
with a long and peaceable joy.

> Anatole France
> *The Connoisseur, October 1911*
> *Vol. XXXI, No. 122, p. 89*

# *Foreword*

In response to the many comments and helpful suggestions received following publication of *Anthology* Volume I, this book will seek both to expand on some of the previous chapters and to explore new areas of broad interest. We begin with a discussion of regional styles and distinctive harness decoration, a topic that is never-ending and will no doubt stimulate much further debate and research. Also, whilst our primary focus remains squarely on the rare, the uncommon and the finest, please allow that several of the examples used to illustrate a given section will be more familiar.

As noted before, colour photography of horse brasses can be most challenging absent the controlled lighting environment of a studio. Through the great kindness of many members who have granted us access to their collections, each of the following 270 examples has been recorded in situ. We therefore again apologise in advance for inconsistencies of perspective, optical distortions, unwanted reflections, anomalies of colour balance and other image deficiencies that may be observed.

Considerations of space have forced us to vary the scale of reproduction from chapter to chapter. Our aim in general, however, has been to show brasses on the same page in accurate proportion both to each other and to those opposite. Of necessity, exceptions have been made for some of the martingales.

Perhaps as is the case with any truly engaging hobby, the accumulated lore of horse brass collecting is so vast that no single volume, or even two, can ever do justice to the subject. Herein we have endeavoured to spotlight certain superb examples and recurring themes from an era long past, but rediscovering history is not always an exact science. If, in the pages that follow, you perceive something new about your own collection or find just one brass that lingers wistfully in your thoughts, then we shall indeed have accomplished our mission.

R.J. Bradshaw
I.D. Jones

# Regional Styles

**Scotland and North East England.**

Of all the regions in Great Britain, the most distinctive and recognisable harness decoration during the horse brass era was to be found in Scotland. Except for North East England, where the style was quite similar, this marked a clear departure from custom in the rest of the country.

Very popular amongst Scottish heavy horsemen were these breast pads, worn in the position usually occupied by a martingale. The brass ornamentation was fashioned from zinc-dominant "white" metal alloy rather than the copper-rich "yellow" mixture generally used in England. Scottish saddlers in particular, as a matter of taste, preferred such white brass decoration. The breast pads carried identifying studs stamped with their names, but examples **Nos. 1** and **2** were purely decorative. Pair **No. 3** was also not identified, though it is known to have come from Ayrshire.

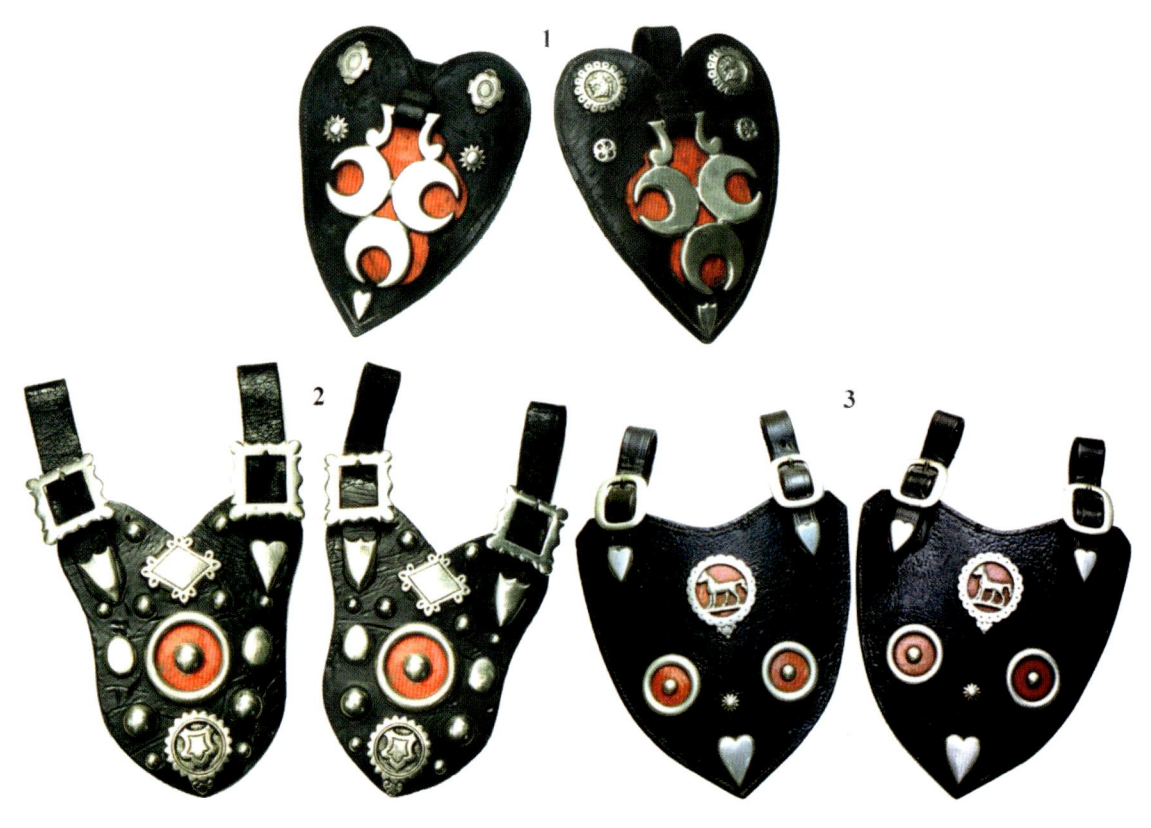

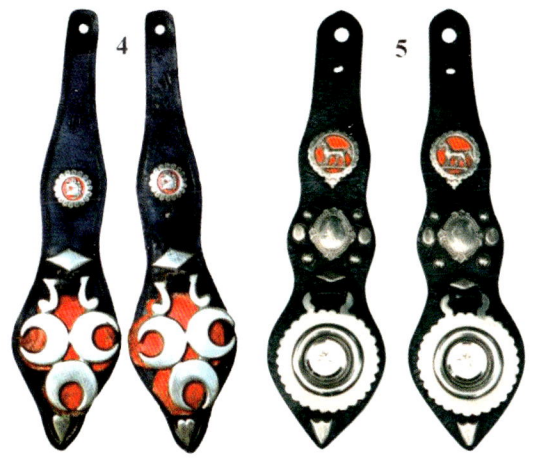

Side straps were mounted on either side of the high Scottish neck collars. **No. 4** shows the matching pair for breast pads No. 1. The three-crescent design is common enough in yellow brass but seldom found in white metal. The pair of straps **No. 5** features rare cut-glass mirror centres. The latter, like their ceramic-centre cousins, were very attractive but also fragile. They did not often survive the knocks and rough handling of repeated use, with the result that any examples still in good condition are now much sought by collectors.

Below, the special Scottish harness style is evidenced by this pair of heavy horses from Prestonpans. Note the higher collars (known as "Brechaums"), the wider hames and the one-brass breast pads, in this case also of the three-crescent design.

The double thistle facepiece in **No. 6** was cast with Scottish horsemen in mind, but this time in yellow brass. **No. 7** details a rare thistle pair adapted for the 1887 Jubilee, also in yellow metal, mounted atop a large martingale produced by Howe & Turnbull, Saddlers, of Carlisle in Cumbria, not Scotland. Clearly the style crossed the border into England.

If the exception proves the rule, **No. 8** is certainly a prime example: a pair of Scottish saddler breast pads in yellow brass. The two studs identify this Dumfries maker as J. Henry of Wigtown. The left-facing 0-6-0 locomotives are rare too!

[10]

Scottish wagoners and carters were not to be outdone in celebrating royal occasions. The superb pair of side straps **No. 9** was made by saddler Jas. Fraser of Elgin. Such harness decorations could often be very fussy, with bits of raffia or coloured cotton strips attached, as well as artificial flower sprays tied to swingers **No. 10**. The latter typically had three-inch spikes for mounting onto the high leather collars common in both Scotland and the North East. Facepiece **No. 11** includes a pristine image of Edward VII under celluloid and, whilst of unknown origin, was made to order for a carter who worked at the Black & White Whiskey Company. Topping off the golden years of the horse brass era, **No. 12** honours the 1911 coronation of George V in white metal. It displays "Regd. 573568" on the hanger and was produced for the Scottish market by William Overton of Walsall.

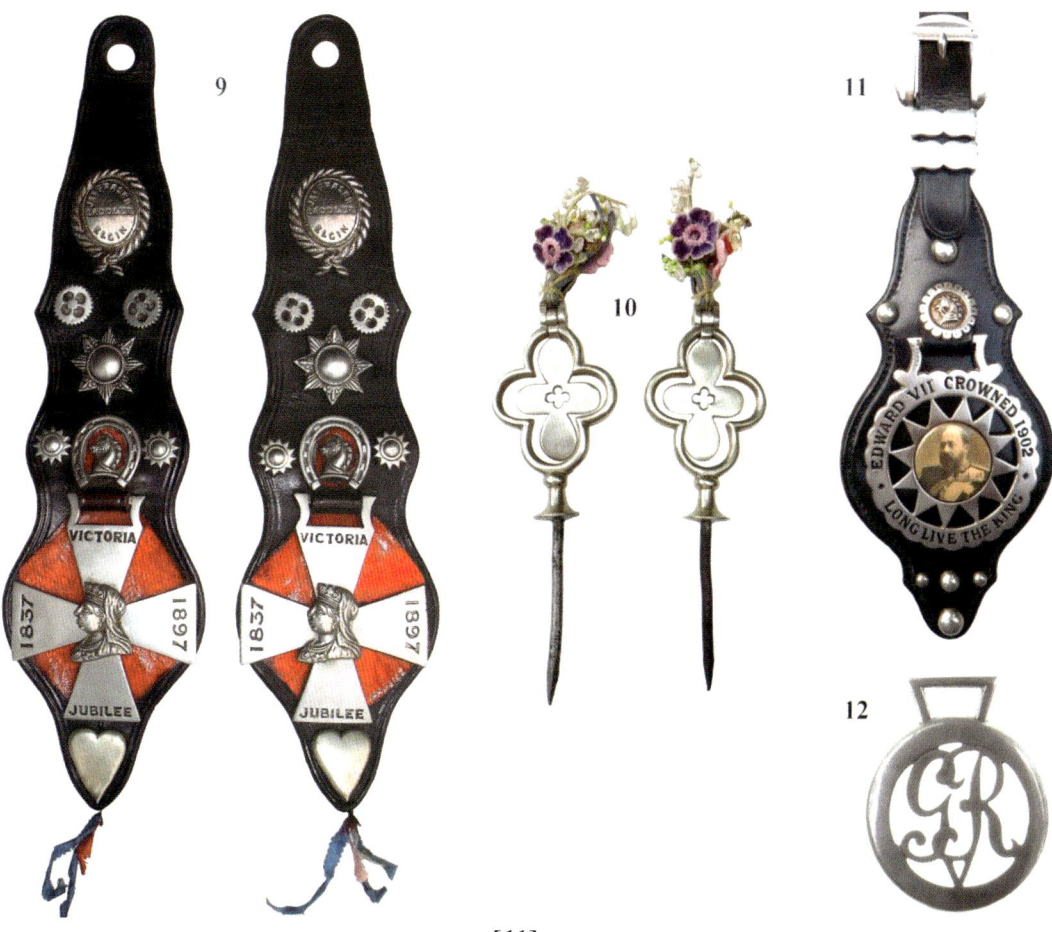

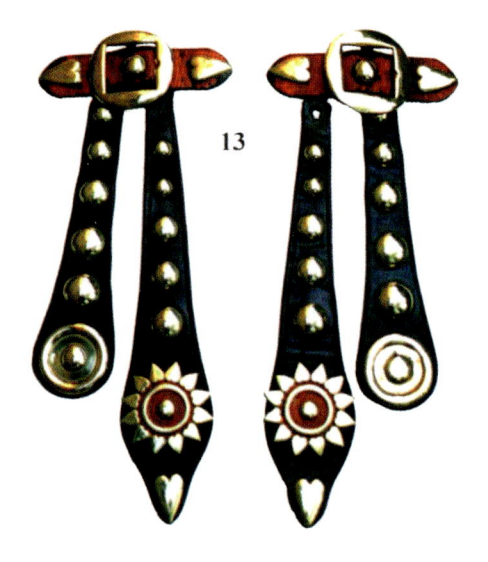

**No. 13** shows a series of collar-top ornaments called "Scotch Stars". They resemble the Scottish style but actually came from Prudhoe in Northumberland and are made from the more traditional yellow brass. Like those in white metal to the north of Hadrian's Wall, these are thinly stamped, lead-filled and attached to the leather by fine wire fasteners. Other designs of such harness decorations and saddler studs may be found in R. E. Thacker's 1905 catalogue "The Four-in-Hand".

The early photograph below, recorded prior to the start of a cart horse parade in East Lothian, captures the essence of Scottish style. Note again the high collars, single-brass breast pads and artificial flowers on wire frames. As time progressed these floral displays became larger and more sophisticated.

## Merseyside.

With a history and traditions dating back to the 13$^{th}$ century, and as one of the most important world trading ports during the 19$^{th}$, it is not surprising that Liverpool also had its own style of harness decoration. This is discernible in everything from basic design to the use of oilcloth and patent leather to the emphasis on five-point star brasses. Known as "Liverpool Stars", the latter found particular favour with dockside horsemen, perhaps because many of the ships registered here had a star symbol prominently emblazoned on the stern.

The special district style is exemplified by martingale **No. 14** and its matching facepiece **No. 15**. Both were made by R. H. Quilliam of Fox Street in Liverpool. **No. 16** displays a mounted stud bearing the letters W. D. & S., probably a local firm. Note the red "American Cloth" and the yellow patent leather edging on each of these examples. **No. 17** shows a pair of star brasses, both with an iron loop on the reverse, intended for wear as rosettes or perhaps as a hameplate decoration.

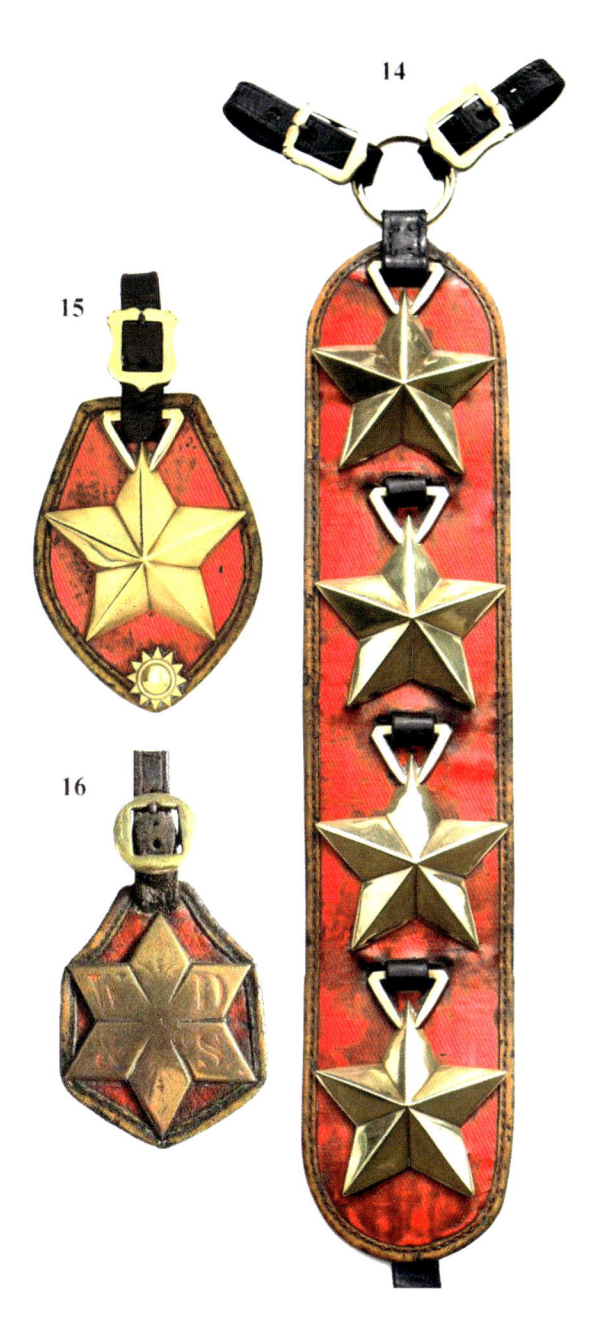

[13]

The black and white archive image below and **No. 18** opposite illustrate examples of the frame housen, by far the most unique and ambitious of all Liverpool heavy horse ornamentation. These intricate pieces may have evolved from less complex designs originally intended for carrying only the elaborate floral displays popular from the 1870s onward. They were painstakingly configured from lengths of hollow ½-inch brass tubing, heated and bent into shape with a tool similar to those used for making musical instruments, and finally soldered together to create a series of circular voids. Horse brasses were then also soldered into place, often with the hanger removed. The finished unit could be mounted on the cart saddle bridge in the usual manner.

These frame housens were a sight to behold at work horse parades and other public events, within both the city and the Wirral district across the River Mersey. Reverend T. F. Thisleton Dyer, in his 1871 *British Popular Customs*, wrote: "Every driver of a team in and around the docks appears to enter into rivalry with his neighbours and the consequence is that most of the horses are gaily dressed and expensively decorated. Some of the embellishments for the horses are of a most costly character; not a few are disposed in most admirable taste and in several instances they amount to actual art exhibitions." Such local competition may provide the best rationale for these ostentatious displays, which were not recorded in other parts of the United Kingdom.

In use, however, the frame housen tended to be top-heavy and somewhat unwieldy. Under its own weight, together with side-to-side movement of the horse, its joints often fractured and eventually collapsed. No. 18 is an exceptional undamaged survivor!

18

[15]

Side panel **No. 19** repeats the red oilcloth-on-leather Liverpool theme with the trademark "Star", but this time in a different design along with other brasses. Typically these panels were worn in matched pairs on either side of the horse.

**No. 20** shows a superb pair of facepieces from a full set of harness made by William Mealor & Son, whose premises were at 413 Newchester Road in Rock Ferry and 78 Grange Road in Birkenhead. As an attractive variant, the brasses are cast in white metal, the oilcloth backing is yellow and the patent leather trim is dark blue. The central monogram, surrounded by three heraldic wheatsheaves (known as "Garbs") has not yet been identified, but both the source and elegant styling of these examples would suggest a possible association with the Birkenhead family.

Top opposite, the Grand Car of Liverpool led the city's 700th Anniversary Pageant in 1907. Note the characteristic 4-up "Star" martingales on the lead pair, as well as the matching facepieces and ear rosettes.

At bottom is an early photograph of two proud carters from the Wirral district showing off a parade turnout festooned with garlands, flags, bells, multiple side panels and a resplendent frame housen.

[16]

[17]

The photograph below shows a prize winner and two other entrants from a Liverpool Corporation parade in 1908. The winner, at right, is dressed with the customary 4-up "Star" martingale. The horse in the middle is wearing a frame housen of brasses similar to example No. 18. Both the winner and the horse on the far side carry a frame housen decorated only with flowers, another style then popular in the area. Also visible on the forehead of the centre horse is example **No. 21**, a rare triple-conjoined facepiece of crescents in slightly graduating size. **No. 22,** not graduated but of the same crescent family, was an equal favourite at the time.

[18]

**West Yorkshire.**

Late in the 19th century an innovative, home-grown style of harness decoration appeared in rural West Riding. This involved attaching simple brass plates to shaped leather by means of prominent screw-threaded studs. **No. 23** is a prime example, a martingale owned by a manufacturer of ceramic wares dating from 1880, Hopkinson's of Huddersfield. It is the selfsame martingale being worn c.1908 by the horse shown below. Note also the typical, clench-studded long shoulder strap and matching plate decoration on the end. These straps, popular in West Yorkshire and much of Lancashire, were known as "Drops".

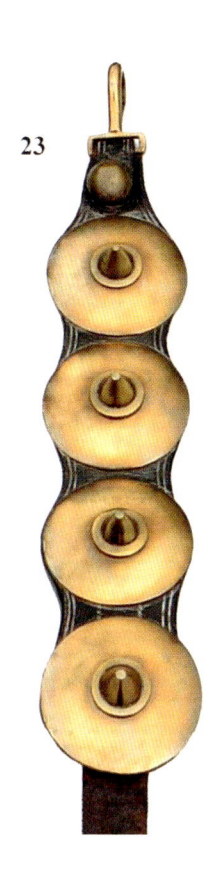

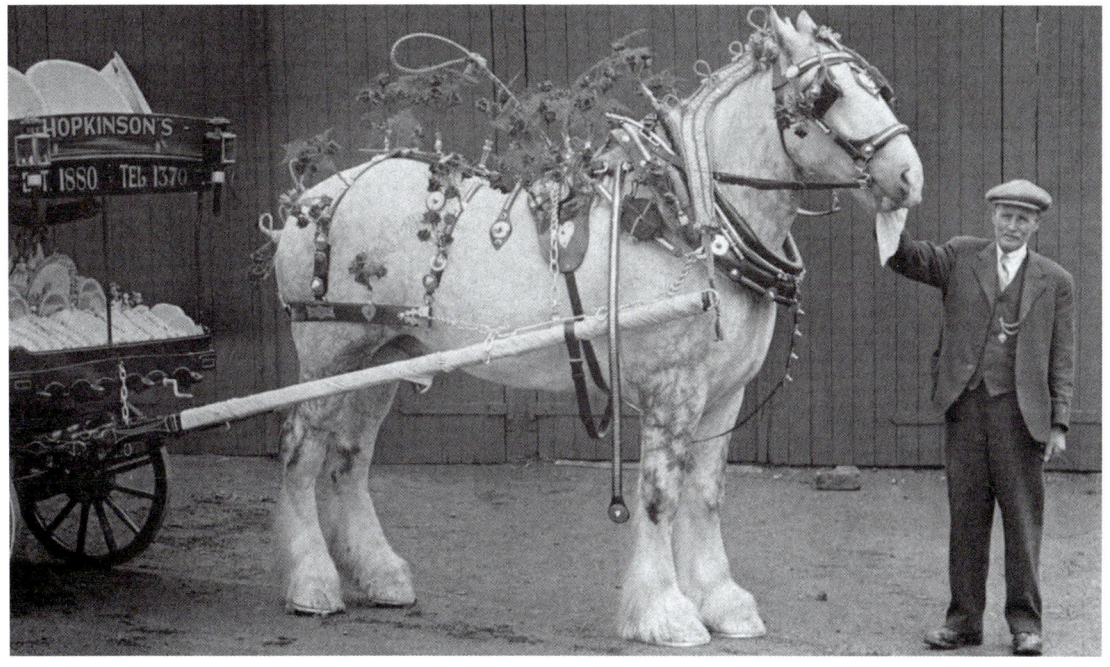

**Wales and Shropshire.**

Scalloped edging ringed with brass studs was common to harness decoration throughout Wales. Facepiece **No. 24** was found in the town of Newcastle Emlyn and belonged to a Welsh coalman c.1880. Loin strap **No. 25** further illustrates this regional style, which was popular in The Marches and Shropshire as well.

Wales also had its own brand of "Stars", as seen in facepieces **Nos. 26** and **27**. Both rarities were discovered in Conwy and likely originated in this area. No. 27 is attached to the leather by means of a large central stud.

**Nos. 28** and **29** are hameplates of the type recurrent in South Wales. These massive 11½-inch ornaments were assembled using slightly dished, graduated "Stars" that needed much careful hand-finishing. The reverse was often leather-layered and stitched to cover the threaded stud shaft(s), around which the brasses could spin.

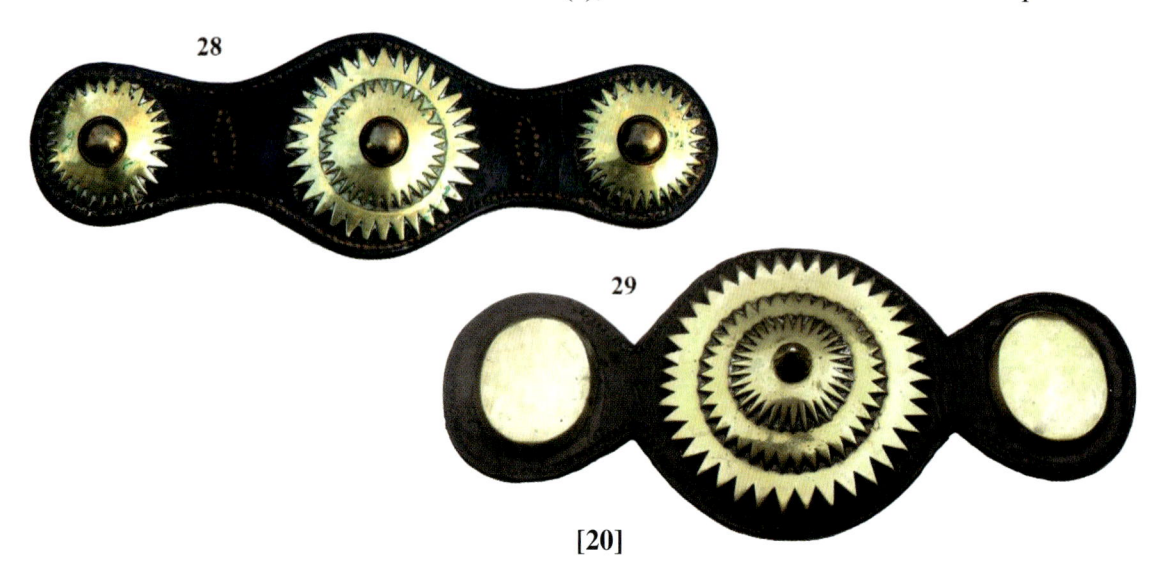

30

31

32

Another large bridle dressing was the blinker spreader, an unusual 12-inch device known only in Shropshire. Rather than being purely ornamental, its main purpose was to improve the horse's field of vision by holding heavier blinker pairs apart at a much wider angle.

**Nos. 30 – 35** are rare surviving examples of different designs. Spreaders were blacksmith-made from shaped brass plates riveted to a wrought-iron strip with an embedded screw at each end. The latter were inserted through a hole punched into the forward top edge of the two blinkers, then secured with iron nuts.

Why such spreaders were needed in Shropshire and not in other parts of the United Kingdom remains a mystery. Perhaps the reason was simply because a local saddler was making blinkers that were a little too heavy.

33

34

35

**West Sussex.**

Any discussion of distinctive regional practices during the heavy horse era could not fail to include the Sussex decorated neck band. These were lavishly decorated, multi-layered leather straps with buckles, usually at least 2½ inches wide, some featuring over 300 brass studs and other shanked ornaments. They were awarded by the West Sussex farming community as prizes for the best turnouts to teams or single horses in the decorated classes at annual county shows and ploughing matches. The band would be buckled around the neck of the winner(s), and the owner would ceremonially lead his horse(s) around the ring in a lap of honour. Sadly, this very special tradition died out with the spread of tractor-farming after the Great War.

The photograph below shows how the neck band was worn. **Nos. 36 – 40** opposite are examples of these rare relics. Note that **No. 39** is identical to the one pictured on the horse, and for purposes of comparison, that **No. 40** is almost 51 inches long.

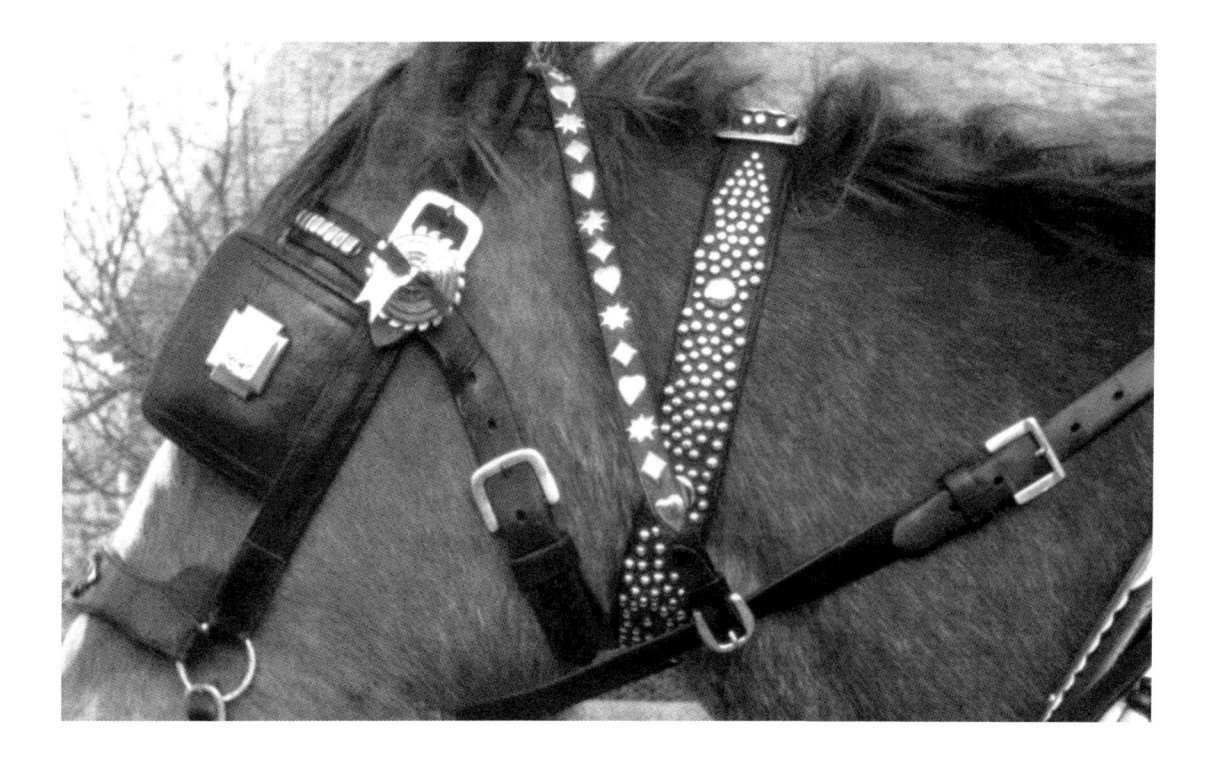

36 37 38 39 40

[23]

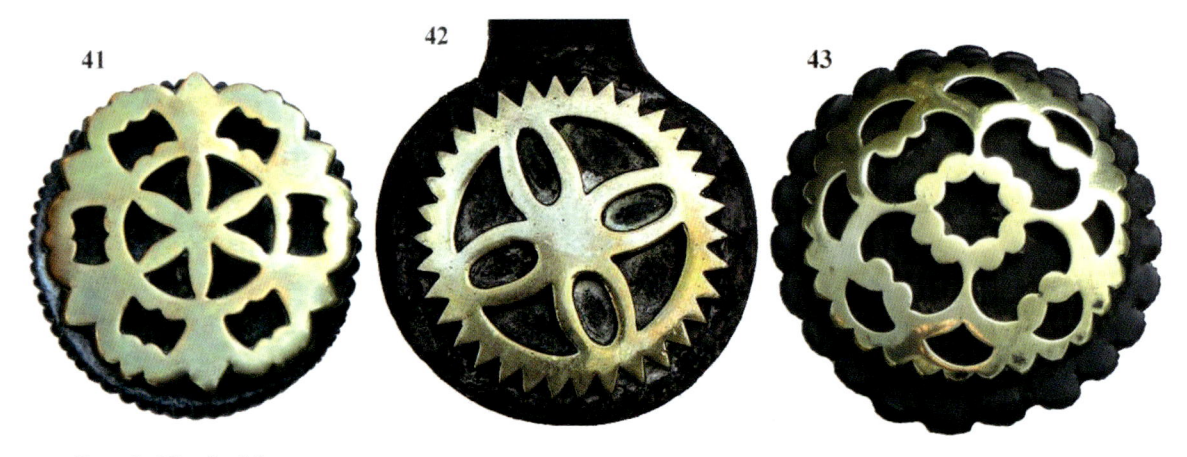

**South Yorkshire.**

Perhaps the most widespread of all regional types was known generically as the "Sheffield Star". Such brasses may well have earned this designation because of their origin and popularity in the Sheffield district, but similar designs were clearly extant in Scotland, northern England, parts of Wales, Sussex and many other areas. Some Sheffield Stars pre-date brasses with hangers and are likely among the earliest harness decorations in existence. Today, none can be described as common, and most are considered very scarce if not rare.

The examples at top are 3½ inches wide, whilst those below are 3-inch types, all on their original leather. **No. 41** was found in Norfolk. **No. 42** is mounted on a Drop from the Bristol area (compare with **No. 23**). **Nos. 43** and **45** are of Welsh origin. **Nos. 44** and **46** served as hame-strap decorations. Smaller examples are also known, graduating down to ½-inch types occasionally seen on Scottish harness.

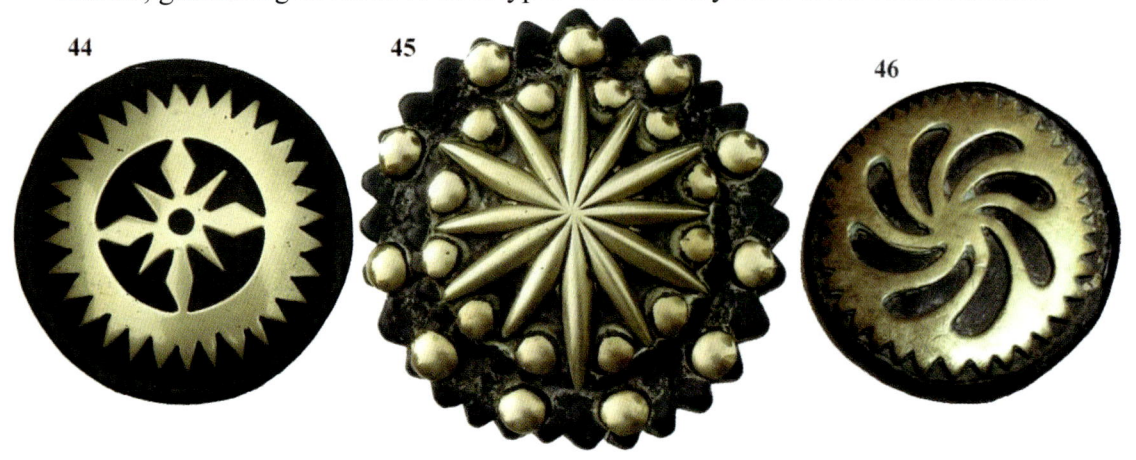

[24]

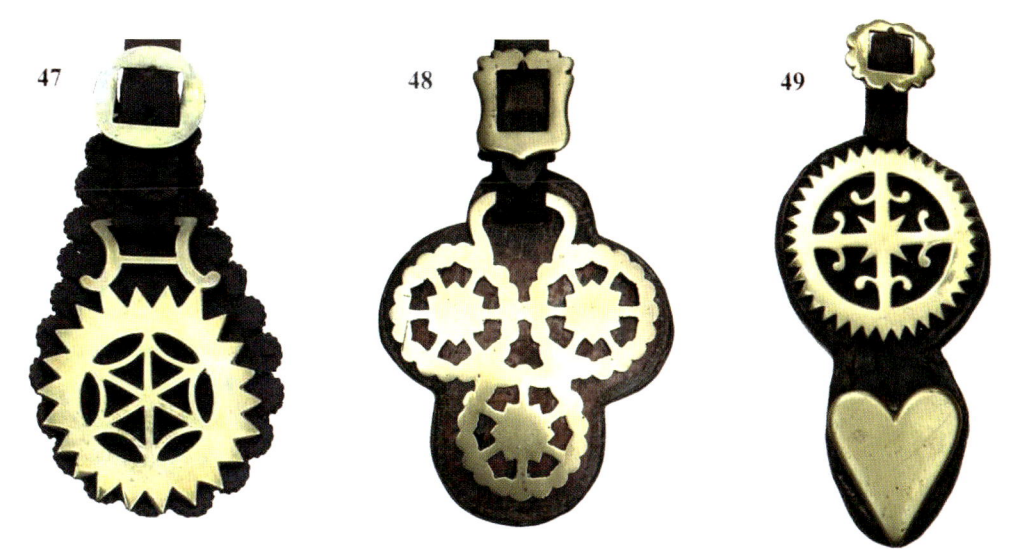

**No. 47** demonstrates evolution of the early hanging brass, in this case adapted from a 3-inch stud pattern. **No. 48** was formed by conjoining identical 1¾-inch studs. **Nos. 50 – 52** illustrate the combination of large Sheffield Stars and hanging brasses. Note in No. 52 how the same cross-Moline pattern shown vertically in **No. 49** achieves a totally different visual effect with a simple 45° turn.

[25]

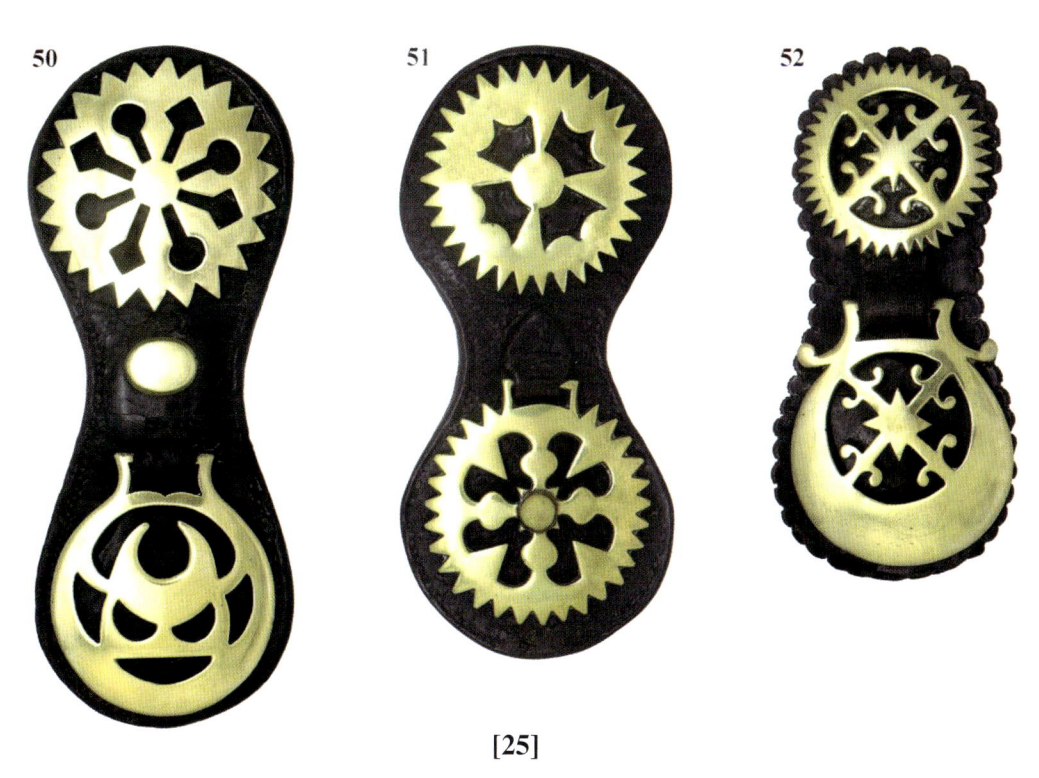

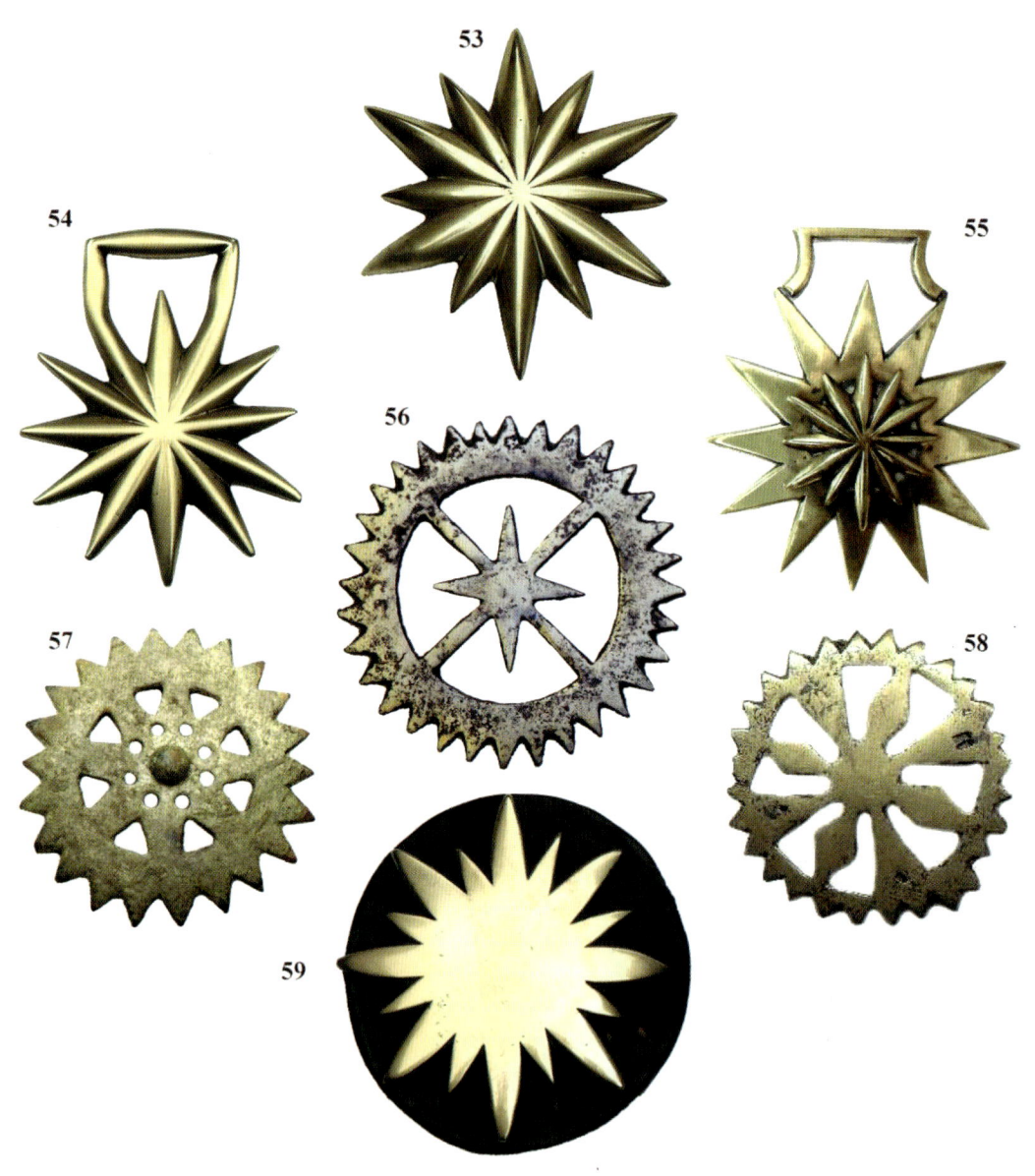

**No. 53**: rare 3-inch stud often used on housens and hameplates, c.1855 – 1865.
**No. 54**: hanging brass adapted from 12-point star stud, pattern No. 348 on reverse.
**No. 55**: another adapted hanging example with applied 12-point star centre, rare.
**No. 56**: found with metal detector near Belper, much staining due to soil acidity.
**No. 57**: previously unrecorded 2½-inch stud, excavated near Doncaster.
**No. 58**: also a 2½-inch stud, detected and excavated near Bristol.
**No. 59**: leather-mounted flat star stud, a likely hameplate decoration.

Like so many early regional types, flat Sheffield Star castings such as No. 59 at left or those shown in *Anthology*, Vol. I, p. 17, have become increasingly difficult to find. **No. 60** proudly displays two excellent flat stars, here engraved with the letter "G". This splendid pair of straps also features two rare acorn-and-oak-leaf facepieces and, as previously seen in examples Nos. 50-52, combines hanging brasses with large studs.

The photograph below was taken c. 1912 in the area of Sheffield. This turnout of two tandem-harnessed horses has just won 2nd prize in the Ecclesfield Hospital Show. Typical for the district, an array of hanging brass and Sheffield Star stud ornaments the brow-band on each horse.

# Awards

Much has been written on the subject of award brasses, more so than about any other single category. In addition to countless articles in the biannual *Journal of the National Horse Brass Society*, available reference materials include four Society publications: *Award Brasses* by Malcolm Andrews, *Parade Horse Brasses* by Michael and Peter Ferguson, plus *All About* and *More About Engraving on Horse Brasses*.

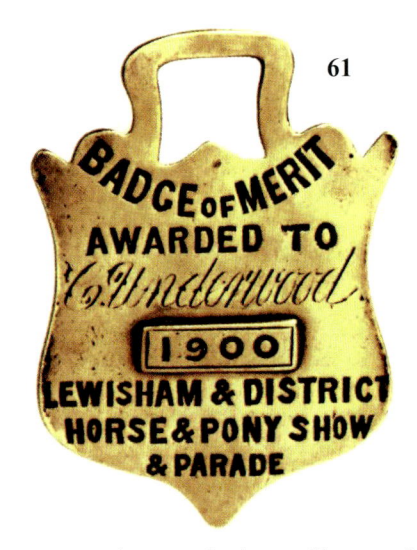

Why are these antique icons of a bygone era so eagerly sought by collectors? It is perhaps because each authentic award tells its own story, speaks to a specific moment in time and represents countless hours of preparation and hard work by the winner. Sadly, it must also be noted, this very popularity—and scarcity—has in fact spawned a significant number of spurious, hand-engraved fakes, artfully crafted to deceive the unwitting buyer.

The award culture was an expression of age-old custom and competitive spirit, concern for the welfare of work horses and, in some situations, entrepreneurial advertising. In the following few pages we neither could, nor do we seek to, annotate the lore of history. Rather, with the group of brasses selected here, from the classic and well-known to the less familiar and unheralded, we celebrate the rich tradition and universality of this convention as it prevailed towards the end of the 19$^{th}$ century and into the early years of the 20$^{th}$.

**No. 61** is a rare surviving award brass from 1900, the inaugural year of the Lewisham & District Horse & Pony Show & Parade, won by C. Underwood.

**Nos. 62** and **63**, opposite, were awarded in 1900 and 1902, respectively, at the 64$^{th}$ and 66$^{th}$ annual ploughing matches hosted by the Middlesex Agricultural & Market Garden Society (viz. NHBS *Journal* No. 40). The two heavy-cast circular award brasses each have a diameter of 102mm.

[29]

**No. 64**: Royal Antediluvian Order of Buffaloes 1st prize award given at the 1899 Worthing Horse Parade, a classic and rare example.

**No. 65**: promotional brass also awarded in Worthing, possibly at the same 1899 parade, from Samuel Clark, saddler in adjacent West Tarring, 1879-1940.

**No. 66**: promotional award of c.1900 vintage, given at a Bristol show or parade by Mrs. Harriet Pook & Son, saddlers of Bedminster & Clifton, 1893-1915.

**No. 67**: award sponsored in 1907 by Colonel T. Deane, CB, former Director, Army Remount Depot for India and presented at the Surbiton Cart Horse Parade.

**No. 68**: merit badge given at the 1910 Croydon Horse Parade, an event organized annually, 1901-1914, by local road and paving contractor Alfred Bullock.

[30]

**No. 69**: 1st prize given at the first Horsham Horse Parade in 1908, conducted annually thereafter until 1914; the applied date is cast in white metal.

**No. 70**: Merit Badge won at the 1901 London Cart Horse Parade by elated carter W. Storey, who had a brass cast to share the success with his horse "Punch".

**No. 71**: award given by the Lambeth Borough Council at their Cart Horse Parade in 1907, strangely displaying an applied White Horse Rampant of Kent.

**No. 72**: hand-engraved 2nd prize won at the Dunmow Horse & Cart Parade in 1908 by E. Richardson, a superb example of these distinctively shaped awards.

**No. 73**: rare and previously unrecorded 3rd prize award from Kent, also with hand-cut lettering, presented at the 1908 Orpington & District Horse Show.

[31]

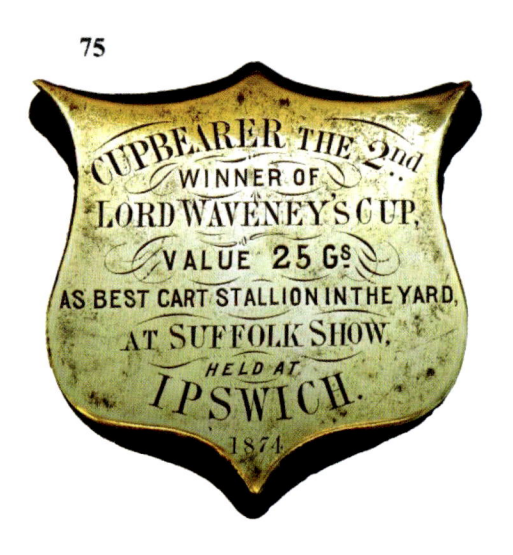

**No. 74**, a pressed brass, was awarded in June 1897 as 1st Prize for Condition of Horse to carter Harry Scarborough by his employer, Locket & Judkins, the London-based colliery owners, coal & coke merchants and steamship owners. The integrated enterprise was so large that this event could well have been one of at least two "in-house" parades, conducted at about the same time each year to promote better care for company horses. An earlier example of identical design and legend is also known, a 1st prize presented in May 1896 to carter Edward Lee (viz. NHBS *Journal* No. 44).

**No. 75**, a 102mm wide stud on leather, tells its own story, grandly announcing that "Cupbearer The 2nd" won Lord Waveney's Cup, Value 25 Guineas, as Best Cart Stallion in the Yard at the Suffolk Show held at Ipswich in 1874.

The two photographs, opposite, were taken at the Winchester Horse Parade, an event conducted annually from 1902 to 1914. They record winner of the 4-wheel-single-heavy class, Frederick John Matthews, leading his impressively decorated horse as he waits for the award ceremony to begin and then, cap removed, delightedly accepting his prize from the Mayor of Winchester. Additional awards, similar to example **No. 76,** may be seen on the table, ready for presentation to winners in the several remaining classes.

76

[33]

The widespread popularity of urban horse parades and award presentations in 1890s Britain soon gained the attention of animal welfare advocates in North America. Starting in Massachusetts with the Boston Work Horse Parade of 1903, such events were held in cities from coast to coast for twenty-five years, until the 1929 stock market crash brought this era to an end (viz. NHBS *Journal* Nos. 60, 72 and 81). The examples above are shown in proportionate size, with the actual width of the "Liberty Bell" brass measuring 108mm.

**No. 77**: "First Prize, Boston Work Horse Parade Association, May 30, 1910".
**No. 78**: "Prize Winner, The New York Work Horse Parade, 1914".
**No. 79**: "Awarded to Prize Winner of the Pennsylvania Work Horse Parade Association, June 3, 1908"; the medallion adds "Organized 1907".
**No. 80**: "First Prize, Work Horse Parade Association, May 30, 1910" (ex-Chicago).
**No. 81**: "San Francisco Work Horse Parade Association, First Prize, Sept. 9, 1909".

[34]

## *Saddlers*

The unsung heroes of the heavy horse era, whose skill and craftsmanship provided the means to manage the raw motive power of our four-legged friends, were clearly the saddlers and harness makers. Located all over Britain, they branded their work with trademark facepieces, nosebands, hameplates and other decorations that have preserved this history and today rank among the most treasured examples of any collection. The NHBS publication *Saddlers Brasses*, an inclusive 48-page study edited by Ran Hawthorne, is recommended for further reading. Here, from the limited number of examples that have survived through the decades, we record a few that are among the more rarely seen. As in Volume I and for considerations of space, our effort is to identify rather than to detail the complete provenance of each brass.

The photograph below shows saddler Henry Hughes standing in the doorway of his premises at 39 High Street in Kington, Herefordshire, c.1905. His brass, **No. 82**, may date from c.1900, before his son (at right) joined the business.

**No. 83**: Joseph Benjamin's business was at 8 Portland Street, Swansea, 1874-1937; this is the earliest of three known brass designs with which they advertised.
**No. 84**: Charles Sankey was located in Kingsland, Herefordshire, 1895-1940.
**No. 85**: William Downes was a prominent Shropshire saddler on High Street in Cleobury Mortimer, 1862-1903 (viz. NHBS *Journal* No. 12).
**No. 86**: John Downes opened his saddlery in Leominster c.1880; both sons Thomas and Wesley joined him c.1895, but within five years Thomas had moved on.
**No. 87**: Oliver & Son were makers at 1 Market Square in Holsworthy, 1902-1918.
**No. 88**: William Rolstone was a maker in Plymouth, 1874-1911; his brass likely dates c.1896, the first year his address was listed as 4 Market Place.

**No. 89**: Alfred Richards was recorded as a maker on Market Jew Street in Penzance, 1871-1907; thereafter until 1915 his company was run by family members.

**No. 90**: Leonard Millett of Marazion was listed in the first of Kelly's leather directories (1871) until 1880, but he probably started in the 1850s or earlier.

**No. 91**: George Langler worked on North Street in Ashburton, 1874-1899; his son, William Henry, continued the business at the same address until 1920.

**No. 92**: William Sercombe occupied premises on Fore Street in Bovey Tracey, 1874-1907; the advertising on his brass is simple, clear and very rare.

**No. 93**: John Palmer started his Mortonhampstead saddlery c.1884; son Leslie joined c.1923 and continued until the Second World War (viz. NHBS *Journal* No. 54); among several known brasses they used over the years, this example was one of the earliest, worn despite the missing "p"!

**No. 94**: John Hingston Blackler was listed as a maker in Yealmpton, 1885-1899.

[37]

**No. 95**: Eli Hallchurch started his career in Brierly Hill, where he was recorded at 50 Dudley Street, 1871-1880; he then moved to Cannock, retiring by 1907.

**No. 96**: Charles Holland worked and lived at his shop in High Street, Bilston, from before 1841 until his death c.1856; this brass dates back at least to 1856.

**No. 97**: John Higgin was listed as a Burnley maker only in 1896, but he may have served earlier as an apprentice in the family business, which closed by 1899.

**No. 98**: Joseph Cutts had his saddlery at 54 Bridge Gate in West Retford from 1870 through 1889; his brass was cast intaglio and likely dates early in those years.

**No. 99**: Harry Amos succeeded his father in their Brackley business c.1884, retiring c.1930 after more than forty-five years; his brass, expertly cast and carefully hand-finished, may be dated c.1900-1905 and is considered a classic.

**No. 100**: William Herring was a saddler employing two men with premises in Main Street, Cleckheaton, from the 1840s until his death in the 1860s; cast intaglio.

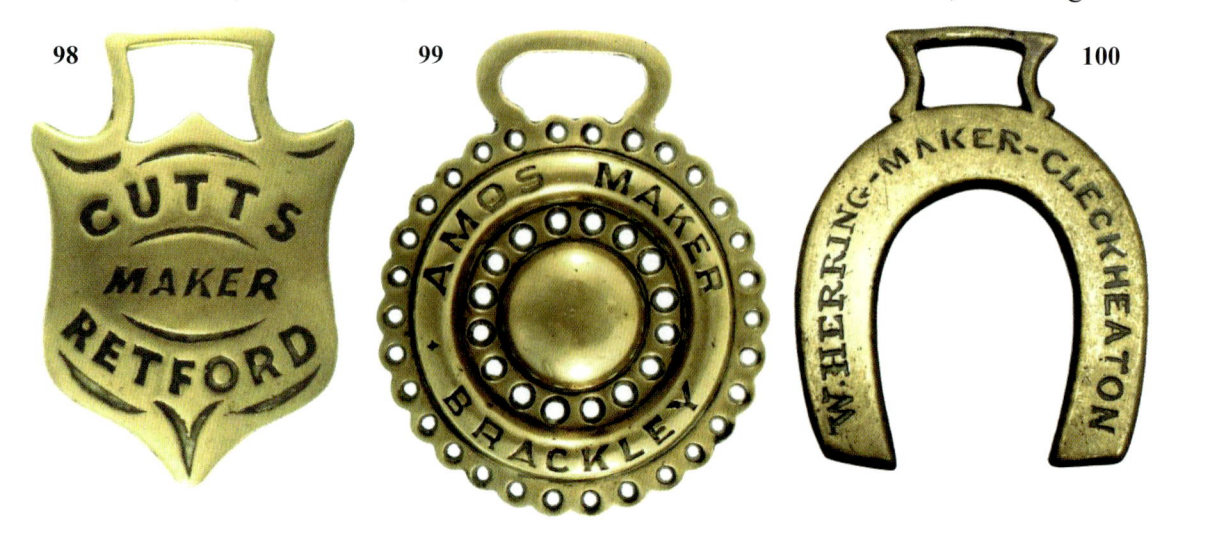

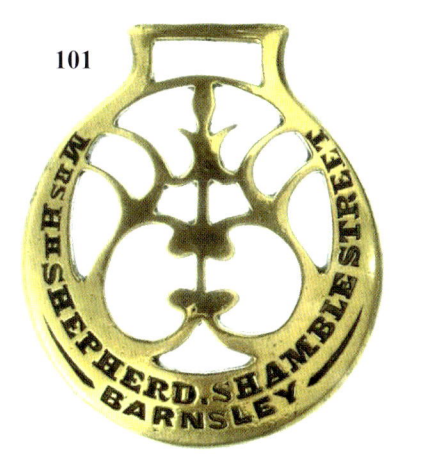

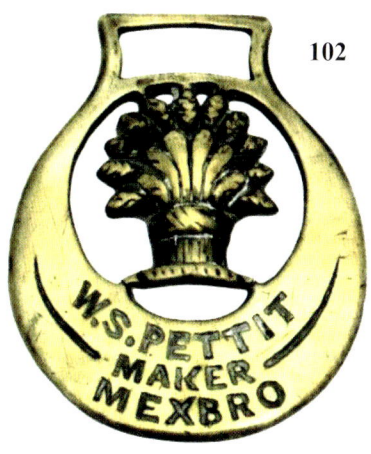

**No. 101**: This brass would date c.1875. Hannah Shepherd was recorded as a saddler in Barnsley at 15 Shambles Street, 1871-1880. Before then she had raised two children, managed "The Yard" pub of the Windmill Inn, lost her saddler husband and become a grandmother. The legend states "Mrs H$^h$ Shepherd", the use of "Mrs" being unusual but perhaps a clue to her intrepid personality.

**No. 102**: In 1860 William Squirrel Pettit started as a saddler in Mexborough. But greater opportunities soon attracted him to Barnsley, where in 1870 he married Sarah Morton Shepherd, Hannah's daughter, and fathered the first of their ten children. By 1873 he had returned to his roots in Mexborough to buy the premises at 104 High Street, shown below c.1890. His brass is earlier, c.1875. He died in 1902.

**No. 103**: William Appleby was recorded as a saddler on Market Square in East Retford from 1871 through 1903; the vintage of his brass is probably c.1895.

**No. 104**: Mrs. Emma Durrant was sole proprietor of her saddlery in Market Street, North Walsham, 1870-1896; by 1898 she had taken on a partner, and the business continued as Durrant & Rushbrooke until 1918; her brass would date c.1875 (cf. example No. 101 on the preceding page).

**No. 105**: Benjamin Day, listed in Magdalen Street, Colchester, from 1871, was joined by George in 1898; their brass dates c.1907, but the brothers continued until 1940.

**No. 106**: Alfred Smale worked on Brighton Road in Merstham, 1895-1933; his brass, of the same design as his father William's, dates from c.1895 when he started.

**No. 107**: Rolph & Polly were harness makers and saddlers at 12 Clarence Street in Southend from c.1905 until the mid-1950's; this brass is a pre-1914 casting.

**No. 108**: Frank Halls occupied different premises on Mile End Road from 1906 to 1937; by 1914 he had moved to No. 195, where he remained. His brass dates c.1915.

## *Nosebands*

In addition to use of the facepiece, saddlers commonly mounted a brass plate on the bridle noseband as a means of advertising their work. Noseband brasses are much fun to collect and generally much less expensive. Always interesting to research and identify, they come in various designs and styles of decoration, fitted with one or two hinges, or sometimes solid.

**No. 109**: To collectors of horse brasses there is no saddler better known than William Albery. Born in 1864 and the youngest of nine children, he was apprenticed to his father's saddlery at the age of fourteen. Seven years later, both his only brother and his father having died, William succeeded to management of the family business. He is shown below (at left) c.1900 in the doorway of his shop at 49 West Street in Horsham. A prolific writer and historian of his profession, he was elected as President of the Master Saddlers Federation in 1935. William was also an avid collector of horse brasses, familiar to many through correspondence and published articles. He died in 1950. The noseband above likely dates back to c.1880 (viz. NHBS *Journal* No. 78).

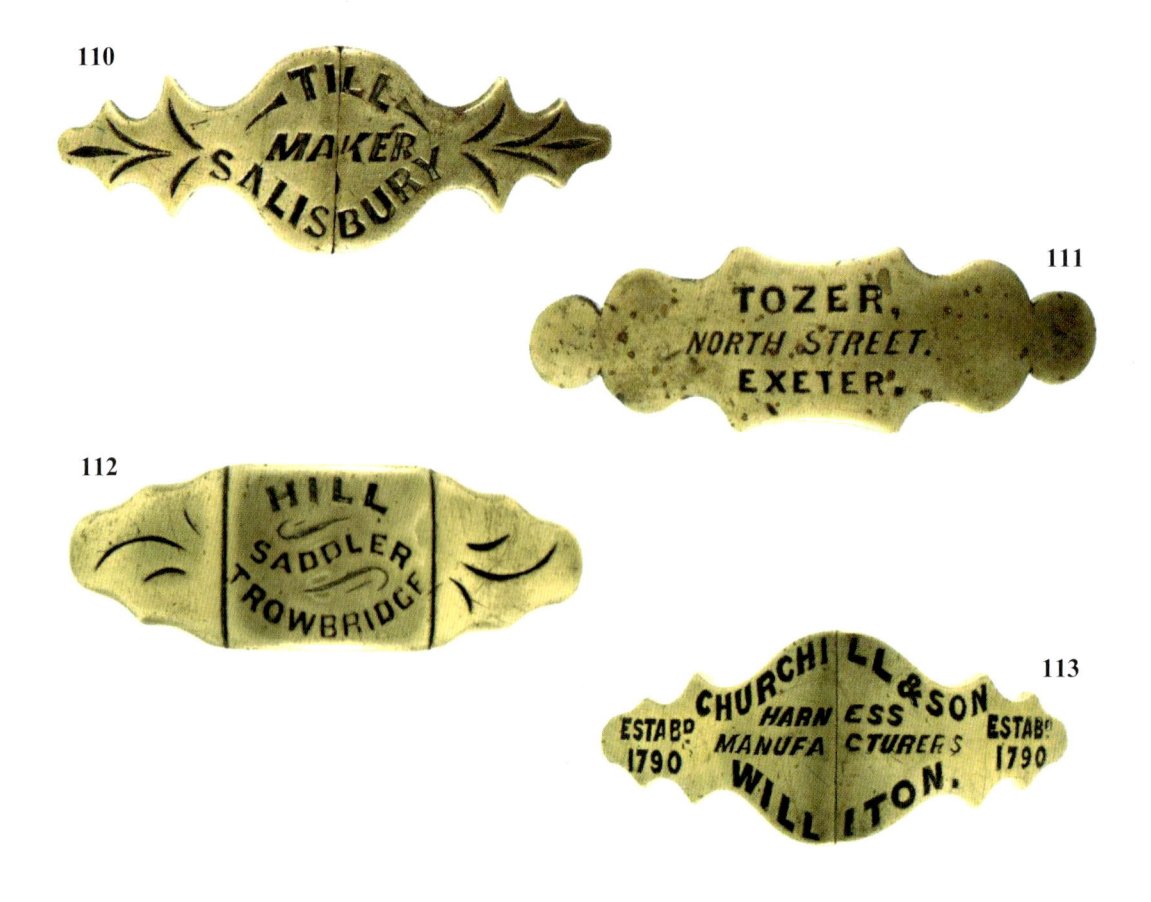

**No. 110**: Mrs. Mary Till was listed at 13 Brown Street in Salisbury from 1885 until 1915; her single-hinged noseband is a superb pre-1900 example.

**No. 111**: Kelly's directory recorded Moses Tozer in Exeter, at 28 North Street, only 1871-1875, but he is thought to have started his saddlery there in the 1860's if not before; the noseband is one of few examples with no hinge.

**No. 112**: John Hill occupied premises in Silver Street, Trowbridge, 1874-1922; his noseband is double-hinged, also not common.

**No. 113**: Henry Churchill and son Walter William worked together in High Street, Williton, 1871-1885, the period from which the noseband dates. Their advertising as "Harness Manufacturers" rather than "Makers" is unusual.

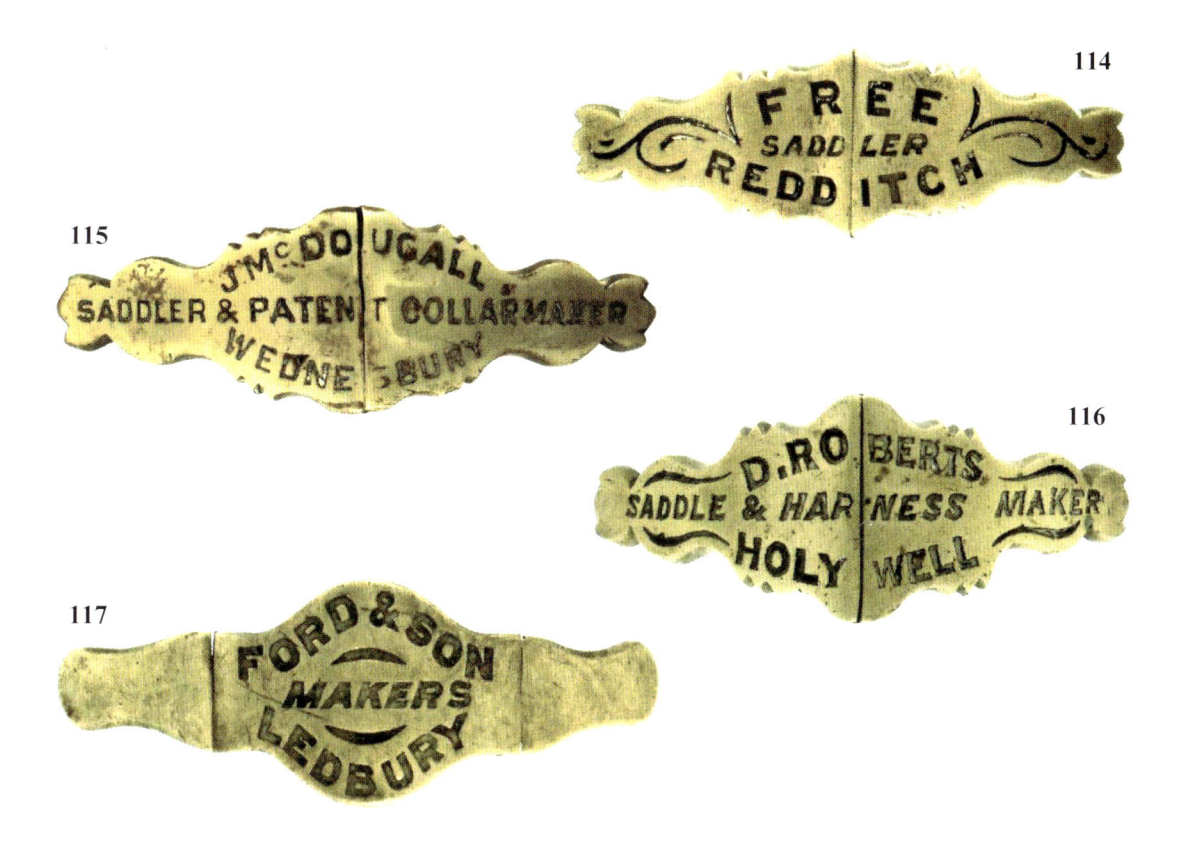

**No. 114**: Consistent with the wanderlust expressed by his own name, William Oliver Free moved his shop in Redditch multiple times over his 1870-1929 career, finally settling at Church Green East shortly after the turn of the century.

**No. 115**: James M<sup>c</sup>Dougall was listed in Wednesbury from 1903 to 1940; the legend "Saddler & Patent Collar Maker" on his noseband is not often found.

**No. 116**: David Roberts was at 6 High Street in Holywell, North Wales, 1879-1933; his message is yet another example of uncommon noseband wording.

**No. 117**: Charles Philemon Ford established his business at 8 New Street in Ledbury c.1870; he was joined by his son c.1910, when they also opened a branch at 3 Southend. Their two-hinged noseband likely dates during that period.

[43]

**No. 118**: Frederick Adams was a young Matlock saddler, first recorded in 1907 at Crown Square, but moving by 1910 to Matlock Bridge in the central, more fashionable part of town. He no longer appears in the 1915 directory, so it is possible that he volunteered for duty when war broke out in 1914.

**No. 119**: Chesterfield saddler Walter Yeomans started 1910 at a small shop in South Street, moving by 1914 to1 Beetwell Street and remaining there until 1940.

**No. 120**: William Hyatt occupied premises at 65 Henley Street in Stratford-on-Avon from 1892 to 1929; the design of his noseband is of 20$^{th}$ century vintage.

**No. 121**: Charles Needham had shops in Bridge Street, Bakewell, from 1901 and at 17 South Street in Buxton from 1902, both until 1922 when he retired.

# *Martingales*

The martingale, also referred to as a breast strap, epitomised the best of a saddler's craftsmanship and artistry. Design of the finished product clearly depended on its intended use, not to mention the available inventory of brasses in the shop. Different motifs served different purposes, whether commemorative, patriotic, commercial, simple identification, awards, or dress at shows and other public events. The number and selection of brasses, the shape and layers of leather, the type and quantity of studs—all these were decisions to be taken, either by the customer or by the maker. With the obvious exception of straps produced for teams of horses or business advertising, no two were ever quite the same. Some were fancy, some were plain, all were highly decorative.

Sometimes, like the stained glass window in a cathedral, the martingale was more esoteric, perhaps a subconscious reflection of the owner's aspirations and beliefs as well as his superstitions, tastes and imagination. Welsh strap **No. 122** is a grand example, displaying a rare sun-star-moon pattern suspended atop a heart and three equally galactic stamped brasses, plus a scalloped leather edging ringed with button-stud satellites. It is not for us here to speculate about hidden symbolism. Rather, we include this thought-provoking treasure because it so profoundly explains why collectors collect horse brasses.

[45]

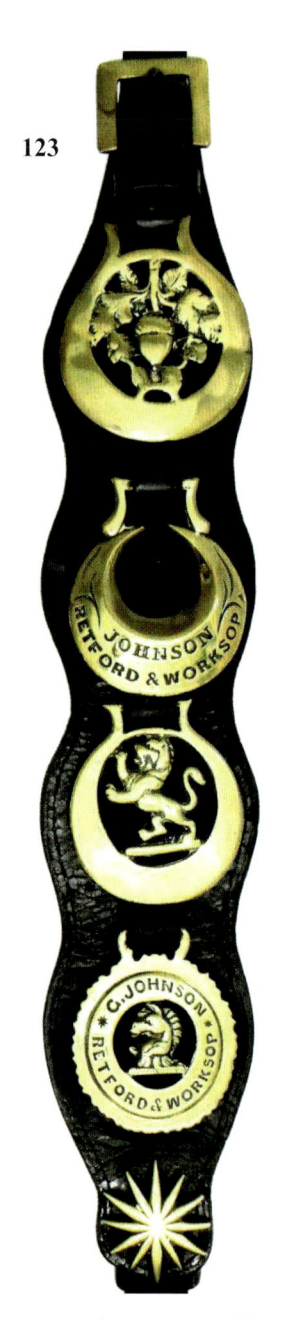

**No. 123**: George Johnson was listed as a saddler, together with his father, in both Retford and Worksop, 1875-1884; such a father/son strap is quite rare.

**No. 124**: leather-layered, well-worn 19th century example decorated in classic Welsh style, probably for show; the bell brass is a casting, the others are stamped.

[46]

**No. 125**: the Lyre shape of an emblematic Mortonhampstead saddler brass was used by William Charles Lavers to advertise, 1892 to c.1905; by 1907 he had taken on a partner and renamed the business as Lavers & Dymond.

**No. 126**: commemorative strap produced c.1902 to celebrate the new monarch; the third brass reads "Let Victory Crown King Edward's Reign".

[47]

**No. 127**: graduating heart martingale from the late 1850s found on an old farm in Derbyshire; the reverse is leather-layered and stitched to protect the horse.

**No. 128**: small three-brass example from the 1880s with a rarely seen "snowflake" crescent at left (viz. H.S. Richards, *Horse Brass Collections*, No.1, p.15).

[48]

**No. 129**: leather-layered 1870s strap featuring two Sheffield Star studs; at centre is a rare, previously unrecorded example with four "Queen's crown" voids.

**No. 130**: not grand but strangely beguiling homemade strap of great age and wear, cobbled from bits of vintage leather and brasses that have been in place for well over a century; this example was discovered in West Sussex.

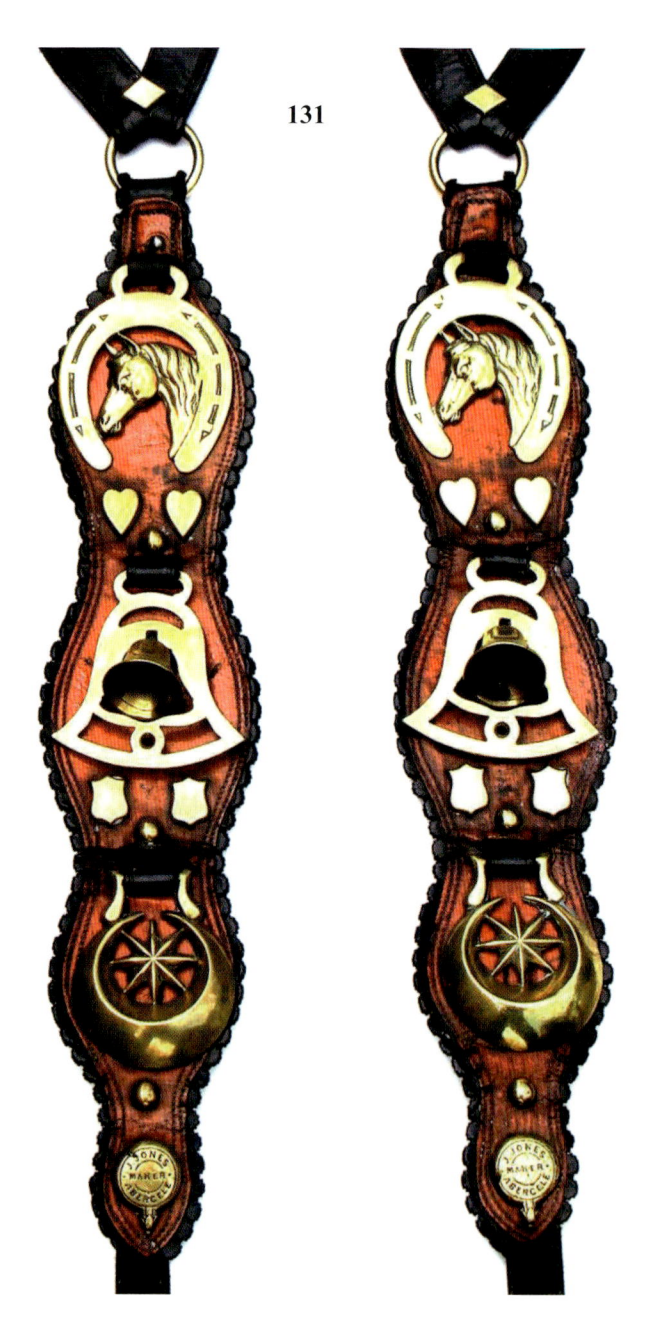

**No. 131**: stunning leather-layered and double-stitched martingale pair, produced by 19th century Welsh saddler John Jones of Abergele, Conwy, no doubt for use on a show harness; the stud bearing his name is visible at bottom.

# Hameplates

**132**

**RAMBLING KATIE**

Mounted on the upper leather strap that bridged and secured the two arching hames to frame the horse collar, the brass hameplate was always a distinctive feature on any turnout. Many different types, mostly 5-6 inches wide, were available (e.g. Hampson & Scott, *Equine Album*, p.47). Some were left blank as sun-flashes, but the majority carried custom intaglio lettering or design or an applied emblem. **No. 132**, with its elegant Titian-red plume, testified to the love of one caring carter for his horse.

133

134

The bell hameplate was more costly to make and expensive to buy, but a popular item with those who could afford to pay because its ting-a-ling sound drew attention. Not many survive. These two 6-inch examples were cast from the same pattern, have seen wear and yet are in near-perfect condition, complete with their original clappers. **No. 133** is a one-off, its abstract motif created by three applied geometric studs. **No. 134**, with leather backing, was effective advertising for this Basingstoke saddler.

[52]

135

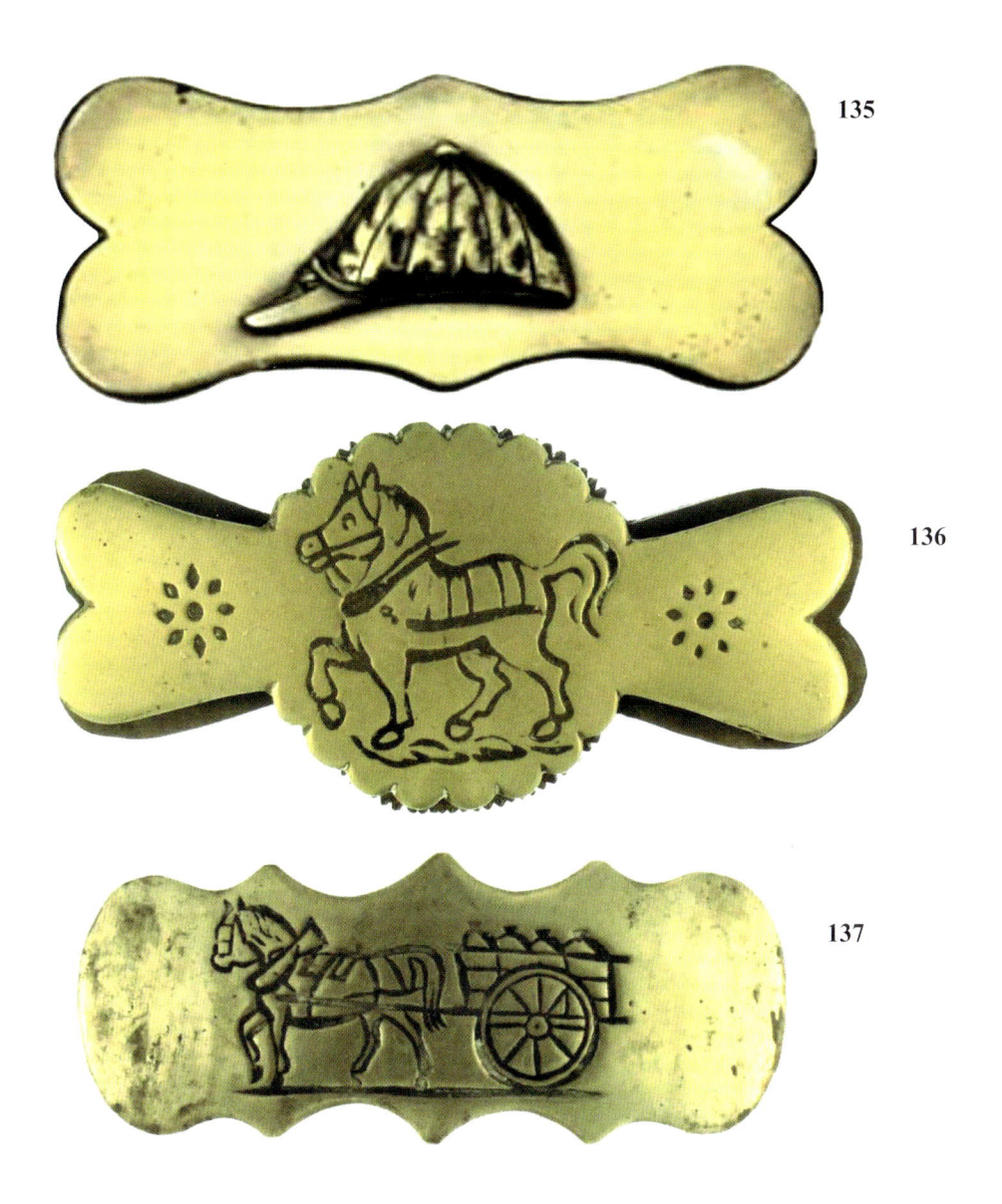

136

137

Example **No. 135**, seldom seen, highlighted an applied jockey cap and likely dates c.1880 during the Fred Archer era. **Nos. 136** and **137** were cast intaglio and are more commonly found. All three are 5-6 inches wide and show the marks of much wear.

[53]

138

139

The broad, flat surface of the hameplate was ideal for conveying almost any message. A double-layered, shaped leather backing crowded with large shiny studs added both size and visibility. **No.138** demonstrates how a standard 6-inch, intaglio-cast plate was turned into a superb 9-inch commemorative, in this case for the 1902 coronation of Edward VII. **No. 139** featured an oversized 9-inch plate, also cast intaglio, enhanced with ten oval studs to proclaim the 1910-1933 business of Bert Shilvock in Bloxwich.

[54]

140

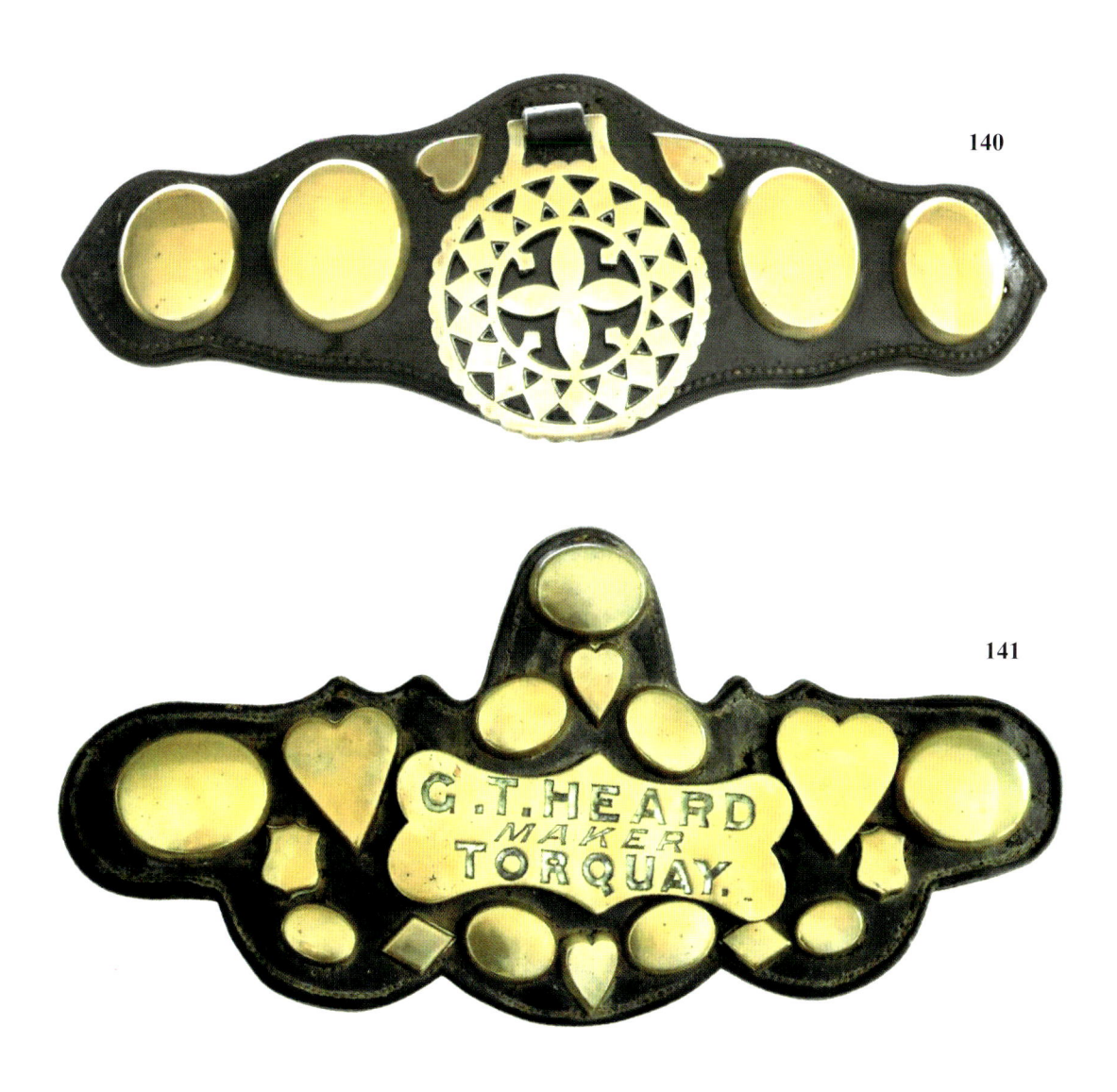

141

The leather-layered backing for the two examples above measures about 13 inches across. A rare variant, **No. 140** employed patterned facepiece #2565 from the 1902 Matthew Harvey catalogue instead of the traditional brass plate, plus heart and oval studs, to create a strikingly attractive bridge for the hames. **No. 141** is a massive, stud-saturated piece created to carry a single 5-inch, intaglio-cast hameplate. Clearly this Torquay saddler wanted to guarantee that nobody would miss his name!

[55]

**142**

**143**

**144**

No. **142**, another saddler example, presents a style of design commonly seen on nosebands but unusual on a hameplate. No. **143** featured an applied "King's crown" and two heraldic horse heads, all with fantastic detail; but such curious combination, whilst attractive, made it neither royal nor commemorative. Example No. **144**, known as the "ploughman's hameplate", was popular with carters on and off the farm alike. This one is both unique and rare because it was cast in white metal.

## *Commemoratives*

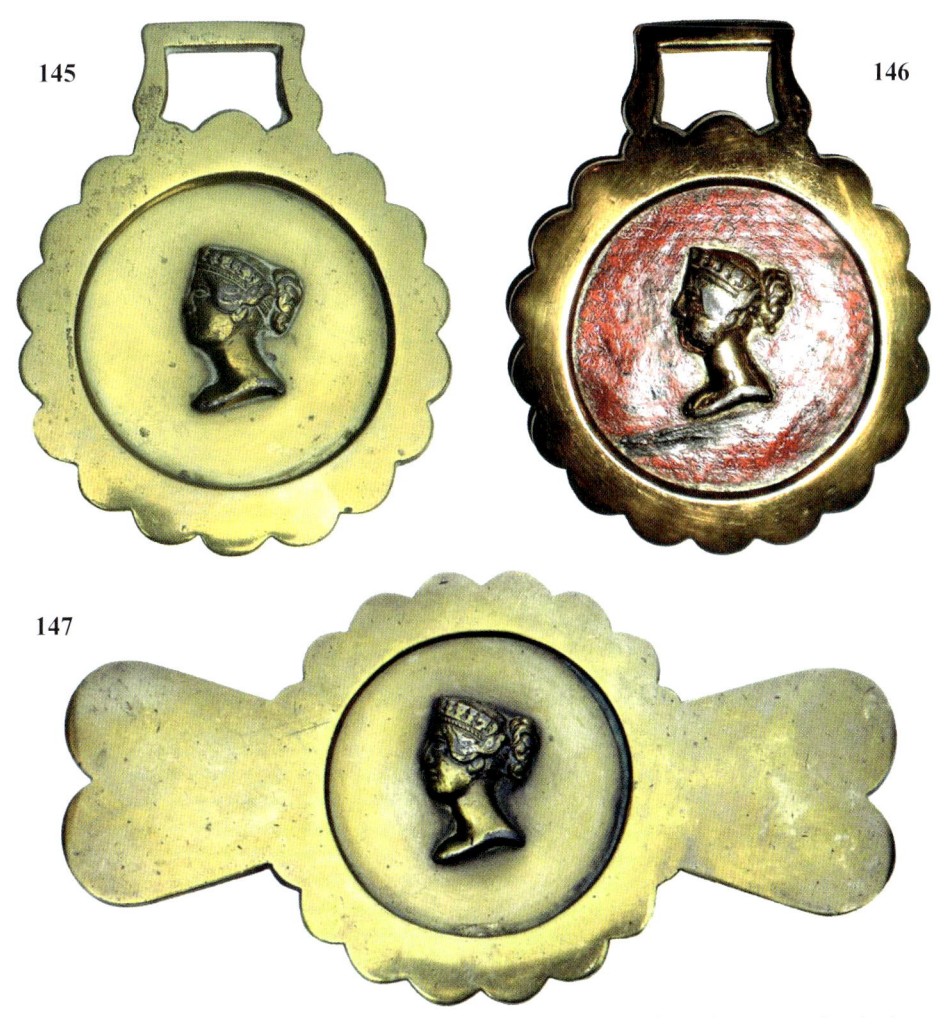

145

146

147

There is hardly a collection of horse brasses anywhere that does not include one or more commemorative examples, whether in the form of facepieces, martingales, hameplates or terrets. As in Volume I, we continue to focus on brasses that have survived either unrecorded or with scant visibility.  **Nos. 145**, **146** and **147** certainly fall within those bounds.  All three featured an applied portrait of Queen Victoria known as the "Young Head", separately pressed and lead-filled.  No. 146 had a more rounded or "dished" frame and a waxed, red cloth backing, still in very good condition.  These examples were produced for the Queen's Golden Jubilee in 1887.

[57]

148                    149

150

All examples on these two pages are also of 1887 vintage. **No. 148** bears witness to years of over-zealous polishing that has worn away much of the surface detail on the applied "Young Head". **No. 149** is in much better condition, but not many have survived. Most of the 1887 portrait brasses, however, used the image of a cheerless, heavyhearted and aging Queen Victoria in "widow's weeds", as shown in the rare pair of fixed fly terrets, **No. 150**, with their remarkably well-preserved original prints.

[58]

151

152

153

154

Detail of the applied bust on **No. 151** may again have been lost, but this 1887 Jubilee brass is a classic, also issued with the "Young Head"; both versions are rare. **Nos. 152** and **153** featured crowns; note the small hole at the bottom of No. 152, likely designed to accept a thin streamer or ribbon in patriotic red, white and blue. **No. 154** was part of the harness for a smaller horse, probably a vanner; the applied crown has suffered a great deal, but the plate has an interesting and unusual shape.

[59]

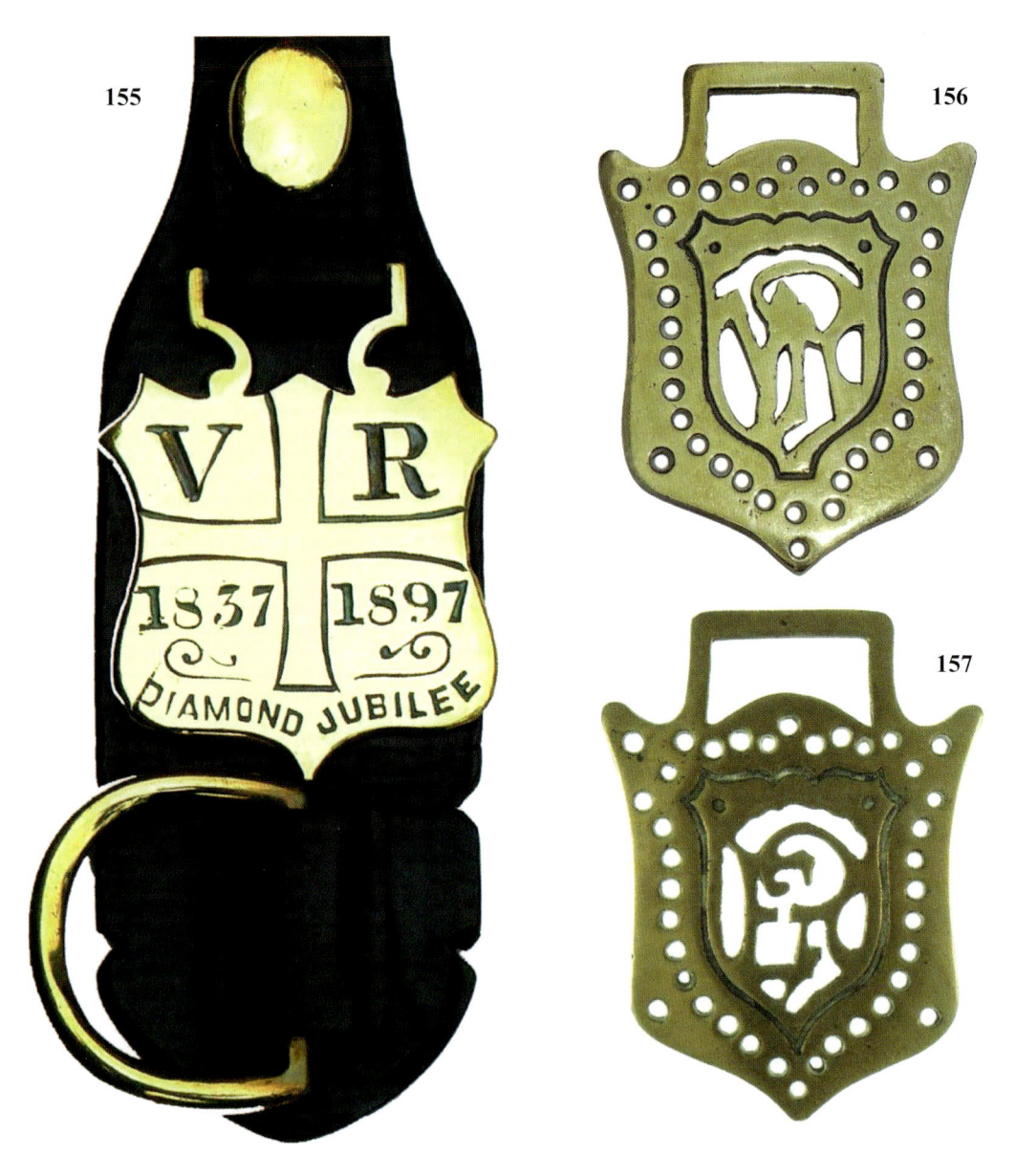

With its delicately cast hanger and intaglio legend, **No. 155** no doubt represents the sublime expression of foundry craftsmanship at the time of the 1897 Diamond Jubilee; to date it is the only example known. **No. 156** is a facepiece produced with a matching hameplate to mark the Queen's passing in 1901; the hameplate is seldom seen, but this facepiece is rarer still. **No. 157,** slightly modified, was cast from the same pattern to celebrate the simultaneous accession of King Edward VII.

[60]

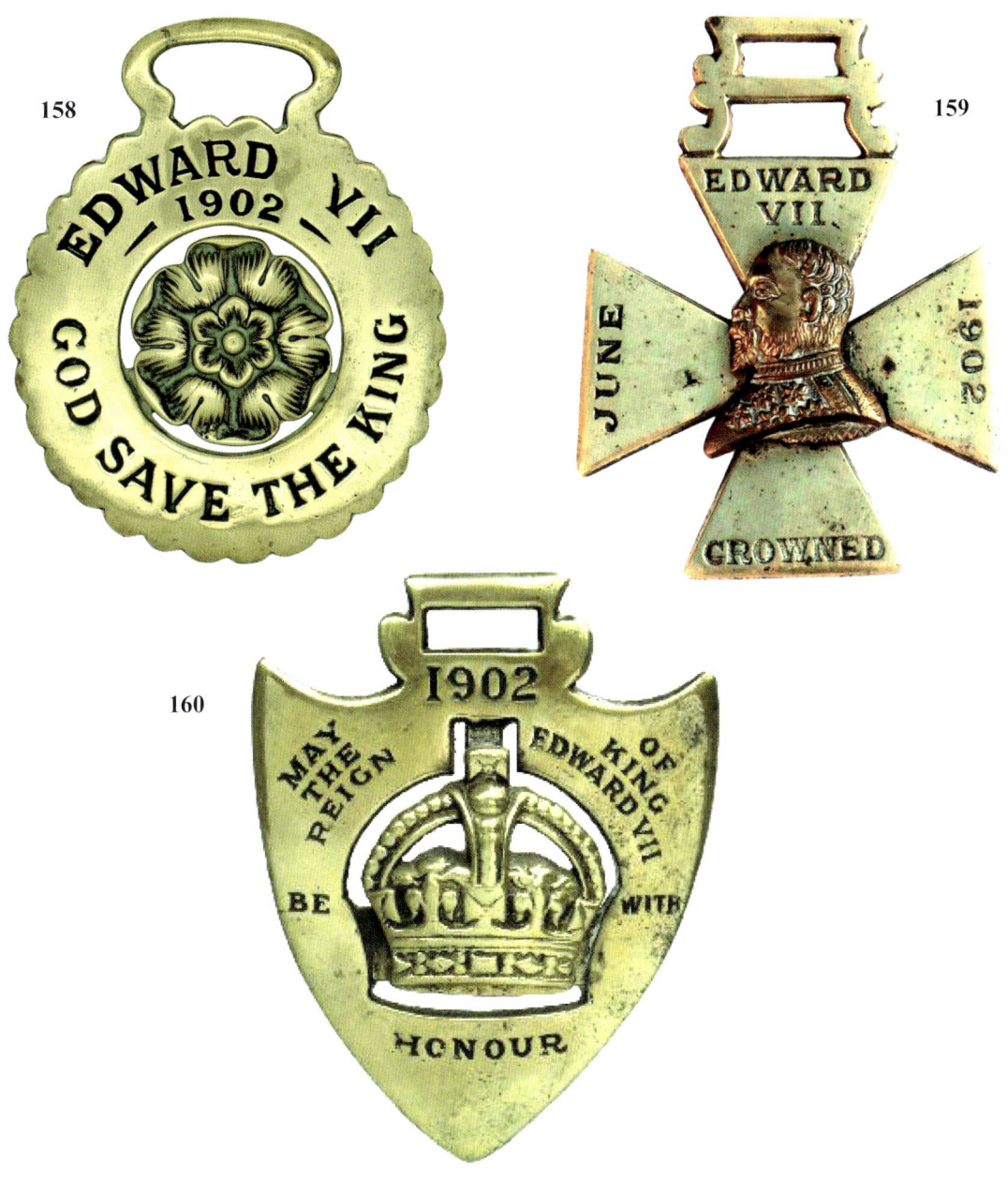

Instead of a crown or bust, previously unrecorded example **No. 158** featured the centuries-old floral emblem of British royalty, a Tudor rose. **No. 159** displayed a lead-filled stamping of Edward VII made of copper-laden "gilding" metal, an alloy of superior ductility, that contrasted with the more yellow mixture used for the cross pattée. **No. 160**, a picture legend brass, included a King's crown as part of its message: "1902 - May the Reign of King Edward VII be *Crowned* with Honour" (viz. NHBS *Journal* No. 13).

[61]

161

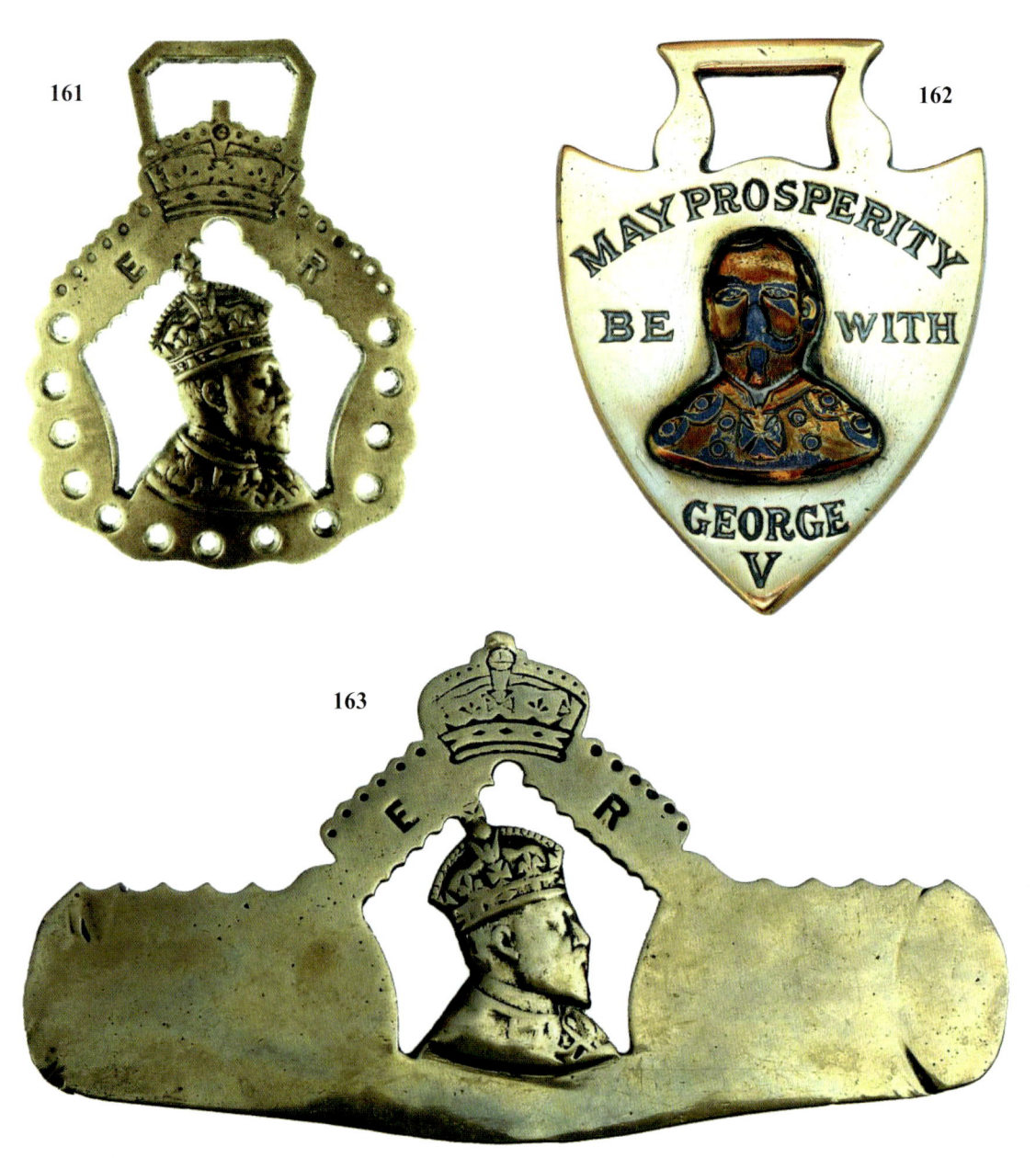

162

163

Every element of facepiece **No. 161**, from hanger to frame to void, suggests the form of a King's crown. Detail on the front of this uncommon Edwardian brass is crisp and well-preserved; the reverse identifies the pattern as No. K33. Matching hameplate **No. 163** was less fortunate, suffering from wear and cleaning (surely by a different owner). Similarly, **No. 162** seems to have been polished with coal dust or other harsh abrasive, resulting in a badly scratched shield and a degraded gilding-metal bust.

[62]

164

165

166

Like milestones along the roadway to history, the above hameplates traced the post-1897 years during the transition from Victorian to Edwardian times, then the abrupt accession of King George V—a period also marked by advancing use of the internal combustion engine and declining demand for horse brasses.  **No. 164** celebrated the Queen's sixty years on the throne.  **Nos. 165** and **166** were identical twins except for the intaglio dating and applied father/son busts.  All three are 7-inch examples.

[63]

Commemorative brasses were also produced to honour persons other than Royalty. These are not common but are of interest to collectors for the history they represent. The above examples remember three men who had significant influence on late 19th century British politics and policy. **No. 167** portrays William Ewart Gladstone (1809-1898) four times Prime Minister and champion of liberal causes; this is a well-known pattern but seldom encountered in white brass. **No. 168** depicts Lord Beaconsfield, formerly Benjamin Disraeli (1804-1881), leader of the Conservative Party and two times Prime Minister; the likeness is surrounded by primroses, his favourite flower. **No. 169** honours Lord Randolph Henry Spencer Churchill (1849-1895), prominent Tory and founder of the Primrose League, Secretary of State for India and, notably, father of Winston Churchill; the design motif on either side of his bust symbolises the configuration of Burma (now Myanmar), whose total annexation as a British colony in 1886 resulted from his order to invade the upper region of the Burmese Kingdom.

## *Brewery*

The brewery industry has long been defined by ruthless takeovers, buyouts, mergers and general consolidation, resulting in the sad disappearance of popular local brands and creating a certain nostalgic quest amongst many collectors for brasses of those defunct breweries. **No. 170** came from Georges & Co. of Bristol, founded in 1788, taken over by Courage in 1961 and finally closed in 1999. A similar example in white metal was worn by a team of stunning grey Shires for which the company was famous. The early 1930s image of the Bath Street loading area showed a pair of Georges dray horses enjoying their nosebags next to, prophetically, a company steam wagon. A shanked Georges stud is visible on the brow-band of the near horse.

**No. 171** was worn by the greys from Shipstones Brewery of Nottingham, established 1852; the company survived until 1978. **No. 172** belonged to Thomas Whiting Hussey of Netheravon, Wiltshire, who was listed in the 1861 census as a Maltster Brewer, working for his uncle, before taking over the company in the mid-1870s; the brewery was sold in 1913. **No. 173** was from Gale & Company of Horndean, Hampshire, founded by Richard Gale in 1847. All three brasses are rare Victorian examples (viz. NHBS publication by G. Williams, *Brewery Horse Brasses*, Second Revised Edition).

[66]

Stud **No. 174** was issued by The City Brewery Company Limited of Lichfield, Staffordshire, and likely dates from c.1880. The company was registered in 1874, built up a portfolio of 200 tied houses and lasted until 1917, when they were acquired by Wolverhampton & Dudley Breweries Ltd. **No. 175,** from Bristol United Breweries Ltd., is probably of early 1890s vintage. This company was formed in 1889 through the merger of four small local breweries and eventually amassed an empire of 600 pubs, only to be bought out by rival Georges & Co. Limited in 1956.

176

177

178

**No. 176** is a rare, previously unpublished, hide-shape brass from Joshua Tetley & Son Ltd. of Hunslet, a suburb of Leeds. Founded in 1822, this company prospered greatly through various mergers and acquisitions for 176 years until finally taken over by the Carlsberg Group in 1998. The Leeds facility itself was closed in 2011, but the Tetley brand has survived and remains one of the most popular beers in the United Kingdom. **No. 177** is an undedicated early crescent with a hinged swinging barrel. **No. 178** is another generic example with barrel studs affixed by single copper shanks.

Example **No. 179** is a martingale pair comprised of repeating studs that bear the monogram logo of Sheffield brewer Duncan, Gilmore & Co. Ltd. This group started as a wine and spirits producer during the 1830s, but were brewing beer before 1860. Later they also developed interests in Liverpool. In 1954 they were acquired by Joshua Tetley, together with their network of 350 tied houses. The photograph shows a decorated company delivery turnout outside one of these pubs, the Plough Inn, before the Second World War. This location is thought to have been near the East end industrial district of the city, targeted by the Luftwaffe during The Sheffield Blitz of 12th and 15th December 1940.

180

Examples like **No. 180** were worn to advertise the potency of draught ale in the barrels on the dray. Four Xs indicated near top strength, but Three-X brasses (and ales) were probably more common.

The "stewed" state of beer deliverymen after a day's work was well known, as was the alleged ability of the canny dray horses to find their own way home. This superb cartoon from Punch's 1908 Almanack was captioned: Rear Drayman (*to driver of dray*)—"Go on, talk to 'im, Mate". Bussy (*in exaggerated astonishment*)—"Strewf, 'Enery, I never seen such a thing before! They're both of 'em awake!"

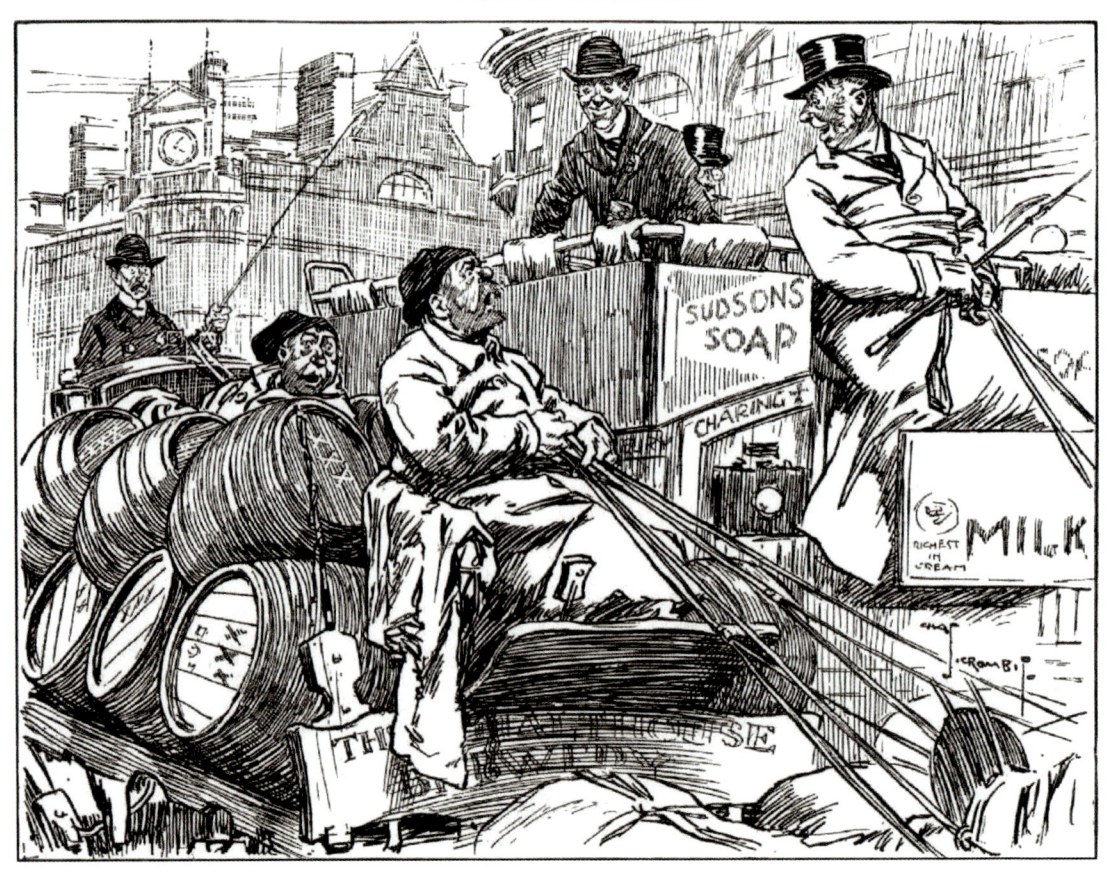

[70]

GEORGE LARGUIR
NORTH STREET
ASHBURTON
1874-1899
SON WILLIAM HENRY
UNTILL 1920.

## Trade & Transport

Fast delivery by motor vehicle is something we now take for granted, but it was not too long ago when even items transported by rail or water started and ended their journey behind the steady plod of a working horse. The brasses in this section bear silent witness to a rare few of the many thriving businesses during that era.

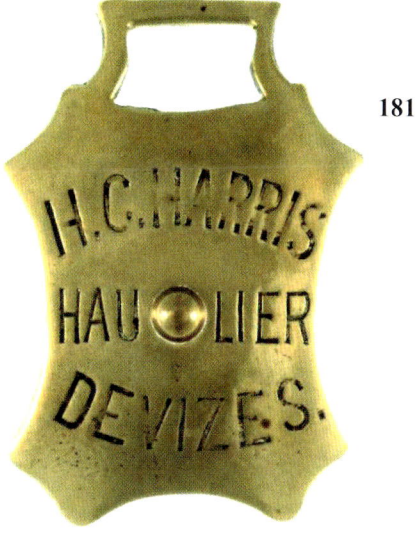

**No. 181**, a well-worn, hide-shaped casting with an applied central boss, identified H. C. Harris, 1880s haulier of Devizes. **No. 182,** a larger-than-life classic measuring 121x87mm and weighing nearly 5 ounces, belonged to Arthur Appleyard, coal factor of Doncaster; the brass was engraved c.1905 (viz. NHBS *Journal* No. 54). **No. 183** advertised for Johnson Matthey & Co., bullion refiners and dealers since 1817, whose heavy horses hauled van loads of gold bullion from London docks to the refinery and subsequently to brokers of precious metals in the City. This company not only has survived but is celebrating its 200th anniversary this year; the monogram of the above example pre-dates 1891, when they registered as a limited-liability organisation.

[71]

No. 184, cast in white metal with an intaglio gothic "P", is thought to have been worn during the 1890s by horses from Pickford's, the renowned goods carrier with origins dating back to the 17th century and today part of a worldwide conglomerate (viz. NHBS *Journal* No. 60). Example No. 185 identified Yorkshire carrier Globe Express Ltd. in the Bradford area. No. 186 was used to decorate the horses of Vivian & Sons, a Welsh metallurgical and chemicals business in the lower Swansea valley. No. 187, dated 1906, advertised the trade of Wiltshire dealer William Snook in Easterton.

**No. 188**, with its distinctive spiraling whorl, identified the horses of J. C. Wall & Co., early cartage contractors to the Great Western Railway for the West Midlands. **No. 189** belonged to R. Lean, GWR carrier in Cornwall; his unusual facepiece displayed a protruding, 4-ring conical boss. **No. 190**, a leather-mounted 2½-inch stud made to fit onto a breeching strap, was worn by the horses of GWR agent R. Toomer & Son Ltd. based in Henley-on-Thames; the interlaced "Os" characterised their trademark. **No. 191** advertised Thomas Lebon & Sons Ltd., well-known London coal merchants from c.1880 until c.1939.

The intaglio "T. B. & Co." legend on facepiece **No. 192** identified Thomas Bantock & Co., another 19th century carrier who worked under exclusive contract for the GWR in the West Midlands. Example **No. 193**, a double facepiece, was worn by tow horses for the Leeds & Liverpool Canal Co. Manufacture of the shanked oval stud clearly pre-dates that of the crescent brass and may well have occurred c.1848, when the L&LCC first started its own carrying division. The stud was substituted for a hanging brass, probably following the 1874 reorganisation of company operations.

## Vestry

As so thoroughly detailed by Malcolm Andrews in NHBS *Journal* No. 18, the local Vestries of 19th century Britain were responsible for roadway maintenance, construction and upkeep of area sewers, the paving, lighting and cleansing of streets, as well as general sanitation in the parish. Such work virtually demanded the strength and endurance of heavy horses. Not surprisingly, the latter wore brasses on harness as badges of official identification.

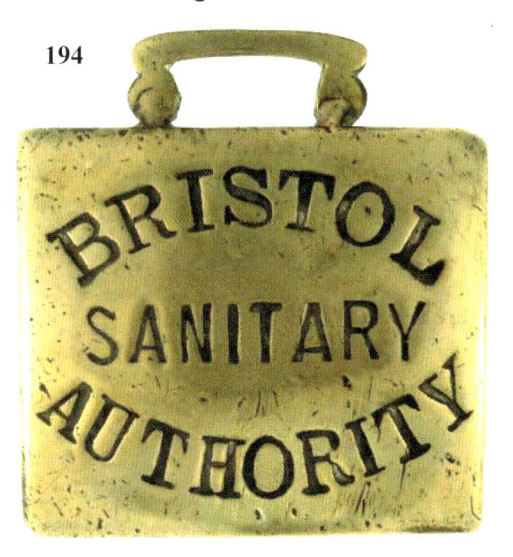

**No. 194**, from the Bristol Sanitary Authority, is unique among known municipal examples. It was originally cast as a 3½-inch stud and fitted on the reverse with six copper mounting shanks, perhaps for a hameplate; but the intended use was subsequently changed, the shanks removed and the hanger added. **No. 195**, also shanked, was cast as the Corporation of London shield, displaying the Cross of St. George and the Sword of St. Paul and mounted on red-enamelled leather. Still today in superb condition, its provenance includes use during a City parade in 1910.

[75]

By Royal Charter of 1571 the towns of Weymouth and Melcombe Regis were merged to form a single administrative borough. The four brasses above, now all quite rare and difficult to find, reflect the maturing structure of this local government three centuries later. Common to each one is a Vestry emblem that symbolises the maritime history of the two seaside neighbours. Example **No. 196** was the earliest, likely dating during the 1880s, before the "Town Council" was reorganised c.1894 to become the "Urban District Council", as seen in **No. 197**. Brass **No. 198** identified saddler John Lake, who had been a harness maker in the district since 1871 but did not run his own business until 1891, the probable year of his example; it remains a mystery as to just why the Council permitted use of its official emblem for private advertising purposes. **No. 199** served as a facepiece for district Vestry horses during Edwardian times, as shown opposite in the c.1910 photograph of a Council employee pausing along the Weymouth Esplanade with his rubbish-tumbrel turnout; note also the two Lake martingale brasses and Lake noseband.

[76]

[77]

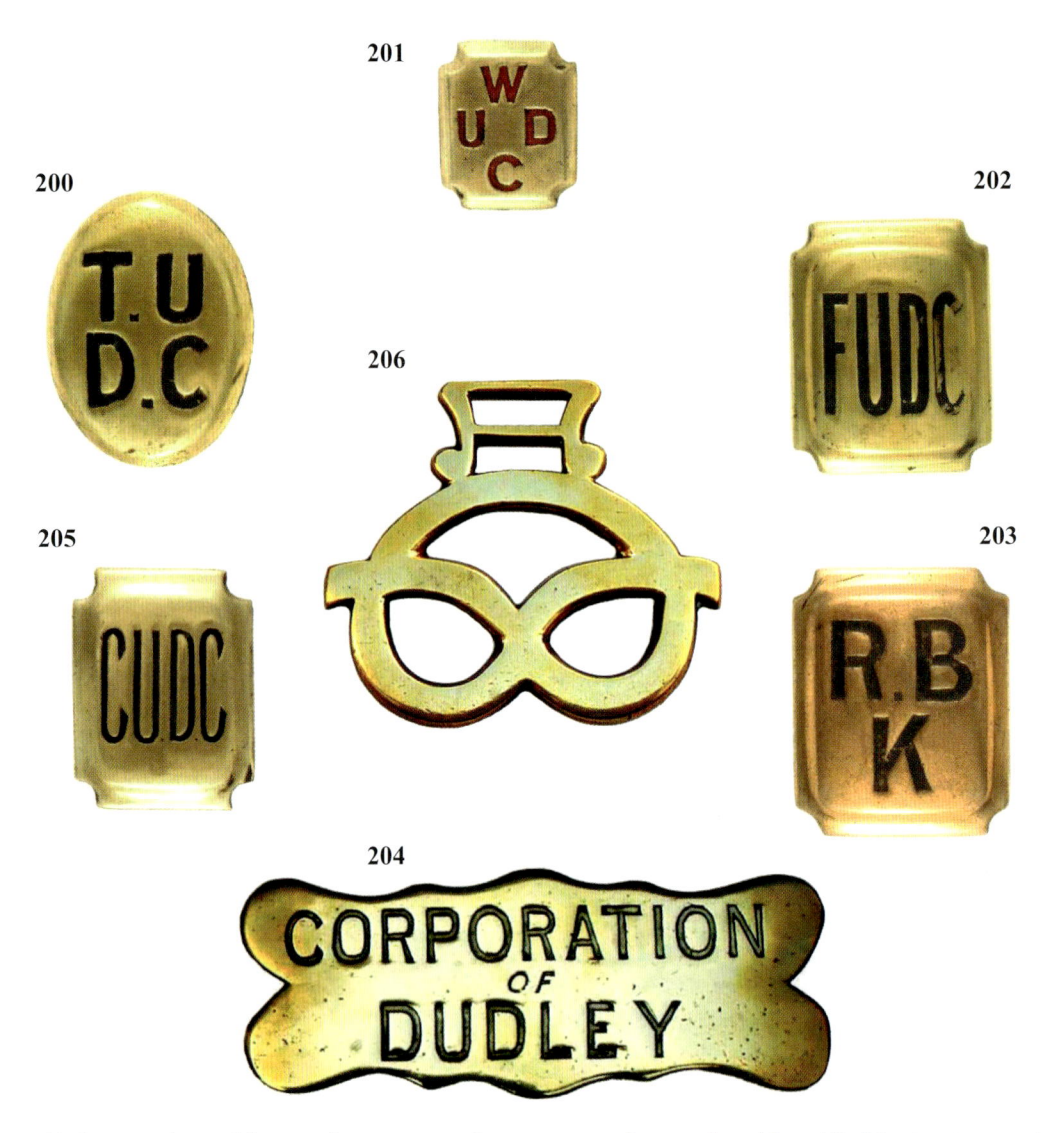

Blinker studs and hameplates were also commonly used to identify Vestry turnouts.
**No. 200:** Teddington Urban District Council, cast intaglio and shanked.
**No. 201:** Westminster Urban District Council, cast intaglio and shanked.
**No. 202:** Fulham Urban District Council, cast intaglio and shanked.
**No. 203:** Royal Borough of Kensington, copper-rich alloy, cast intaglio and shanked.
**No. 204:** 5-inch hameplate heralded the Corporation of Dudley in the West Midlands.
**No. 205:** Croyden Urban District Council, cast intaglio and shanked.
**No. 206:** stylized Staffordshire Knot worn by horses of the Stafford Borough Council.

[78]

# Owner & Farmer Brasses

Personalised brasses, custom-inscribed for individuals who owned horses either to work the land or to pull their carts and carriages, were a common sight on harness throughout the Victorian and Edwardian eras. Most were hand-engraved as one-offs by skilled local artisans but when justified by quantity, intaglio-cast examples were also produced. These brasses are fun to collect and certainly add interest to any collection. Yet determining the specific provenance for many can often be frustrating, even impossible. The two examples below illustrate this dilemma.

**No. 207** was hand-engraved and gave name, date and place. Census and BMD records reveal that it belonged to Alfred Sidney Weaver, who lived his entire life in the Somerset village of Chewton Mendip—born 1865, married 1899 and died 1904. In 1891 he was employed as a blacksmith, but ten years later his profession was listed as an independent "haulier". Why the 1897 dating? One plausible explanation is that this was the year he changed occupation, so the brass was needed for his new turnout.

By contrast, example **No. 208** is a giant question mark. A superb early 1900s brass, it nevertheless carries only the initials "W.L.A.", cast intaglio. This is insufficient basis for further research and, sadly therefore, its history remains shrouded in obscurity.

**No. 209:** Born in 1820, Thomas Wilton lived in the parish of Walcot, a suburb of Bath. In 1841 his occupation was recorded as "labourer"; by 1851 he had established a business as "coal haulier", probably during 1849.

**No. 210:** Silas Charles Burt was a Salisbury wheelwright, 1867-1895; cast intaglio.

**No. 211:** Samuel Benjamin Hathway grew up helping his father to farm 15 acres at Goose Green in Frampton Cotterell, South Gloucestershire. According to the 1871 census for the area, at age 36 he was recorded as working 50 acres at the New Inn Farm where he lived with his wife, infant son and two servants. His Lion Rampant brass seems highly appropriate for such a successful young man. Note that the engraver misspelled "Cotterell".

**No. 212:** Except for his choice of hearts, W. Haines left no clues for posterity.

**No. 213:** Henry Wansborough was a wealthy Wiltshire farmer of 960 acres in Charlton, near Pewsey, where he lived with his wife and son; in his employ on the farm were eight men and seven boys, plus two house servants. The brass bears his name and the date of 1867, just after his 60th birthday.

**No. 214:** "JHP 1878" was the inscription; both age of the brass and style of letters suggest this to be the year of engraving, but further provenance is unknown.

**No. 215:** James Taylor Esq., born in 1858, lived with his widowed mother and older sister on a Wiltshire farm of 950 acres in Stanton St. Bernard, near Devizes; the staff included 18 men, 11 boys, a cook and a housemaid. His brass was cast intaglio and likely to have been a gift for his 50th birthday in 1908.

**No. 216:** "JHT" was the elaborate monogram; the history remains an enigma.

# War and Peace

Napoleon and Eugenie, **No. 217**, is likely the oldest example in this section, said to commemorate the exile and ensuing residence in England of the French Emperor Louis Napoleon III and his wife Eugenie after his disastrous defeat and capture at the Battle of Sedan during the 1870-1871 Franco-Prussian War. The deposed couple lived at Camden Place in Chislehurst until Louis' death in 1873. There is some debate as to whether the brass may instead depict Queen Victoria and Prince Albert, but most collectors do not share this opinion because of the distinctive hair and beard fashions portrayed.

R.S.S. Baden-Powell, **No. 218**, frames the bust of Robert Stephenson Smyth Baden-Powell, defender and hero of Mafeking, the South African town which survived a 217-day siege by superior forces from October 1899 to May 1900 during the Second Boer War. News reaching London that reinforcements had arrived to break the siege touched off a vast outpouring of relief and ecstatic joy. Public celebrations throughout Britain inspired production of patriotic flag pins, badges and this rare horse brass, which may be found with or without the patent registration (No. 357452) on the reverse. Baden-Powell subsequently went on to even greater fame by founding what ultimately became the international Boy Scout Movement.

219

In his *All About Horse Brasses* (1943, p.48) H. S. Richards records example **No. 219**, Joseph Chamberlain, as being "made to the order of a South African farmer" in commemoration of the British Colonial Secretary's 1903 visit to the newly unified Republic after conclusion of the 1899-1902 Boer War. Detail of the casting is excellent, complete with Chamberlain's monocle and trademark lapel orchid. A second version of this historic brass, without the pressed legend, is also known.

**No. 220** celebrates the independent Irish Irish Free State, established under the Anglo-Irish Treaty of December 1921, which brought an end to the 3-year War of Independence between the forces of the self-proclaimed Irish Republic and those of the British Crown. A similar example appears in H. S. Richards *Horse Brass Collections*, No.1, p.16, but without the date. This brass is very rare.

220

[83]

Example **No. 221**, from the British Red Cross Society, was worn by ambulance horses transferring wounded men from the docks in Harwich harbour to the many hospitals serving the local area during the 1914-1918 Great War.

**No. 222**, the Victory Martingale, proudly displayed three brasses that celebrated both the victory and the peace after Armistice Day on 11ᵗʰ November 1918. Each "Victory" still has all of its original enamel intact, a condition now very difficult to find. This superb harness decoration would surely have added colour as well as distinction to any horseman's turnout!

# Noah's Ark

The profusion of brasses depicting horses, animals, birds and fish offers the collector so inclined the opportunity to build a virtual menagerie of wildlife. Examples may be found ranging from the ordinary to the exotic, from cat, cow and squirrel to peacock, armadillo and wild boar. Some of these are of 20th century origin, perhaps "made for the collector", and therefore fall beyond the scope of these pages. Our focus here remains on the early, the unusual and the rare. Double facepiece **No. 223** features Alice and Jumbo as a pair. Castings with three smiles under their names are much harder to find than those without.

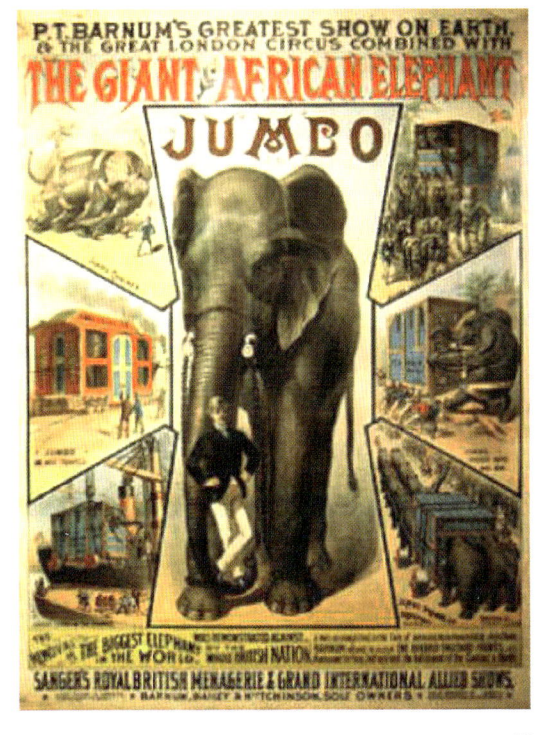

223

[85]

Apart from horses and lions, perhaps the most popular member of the animal kingdom to be immortalized in brass was the elephant. Public fascination with these gentle giants came alive as the result of traveling circuses in the 19th century.

**No. 224:** meticulously detailed casting fitted with both hanger and wire shanks, likely adapted from a pattern originally intended as a stud; very rare.
**No. 225:** most elephants are portrayed facing left; this one, c.1890-1900, is unusual.
**No. 226:** slightly smaller than its right-facing companion, but otherwise perfectly proportioned and well-detailed; also of c.1890-1900 vintage.

[86]

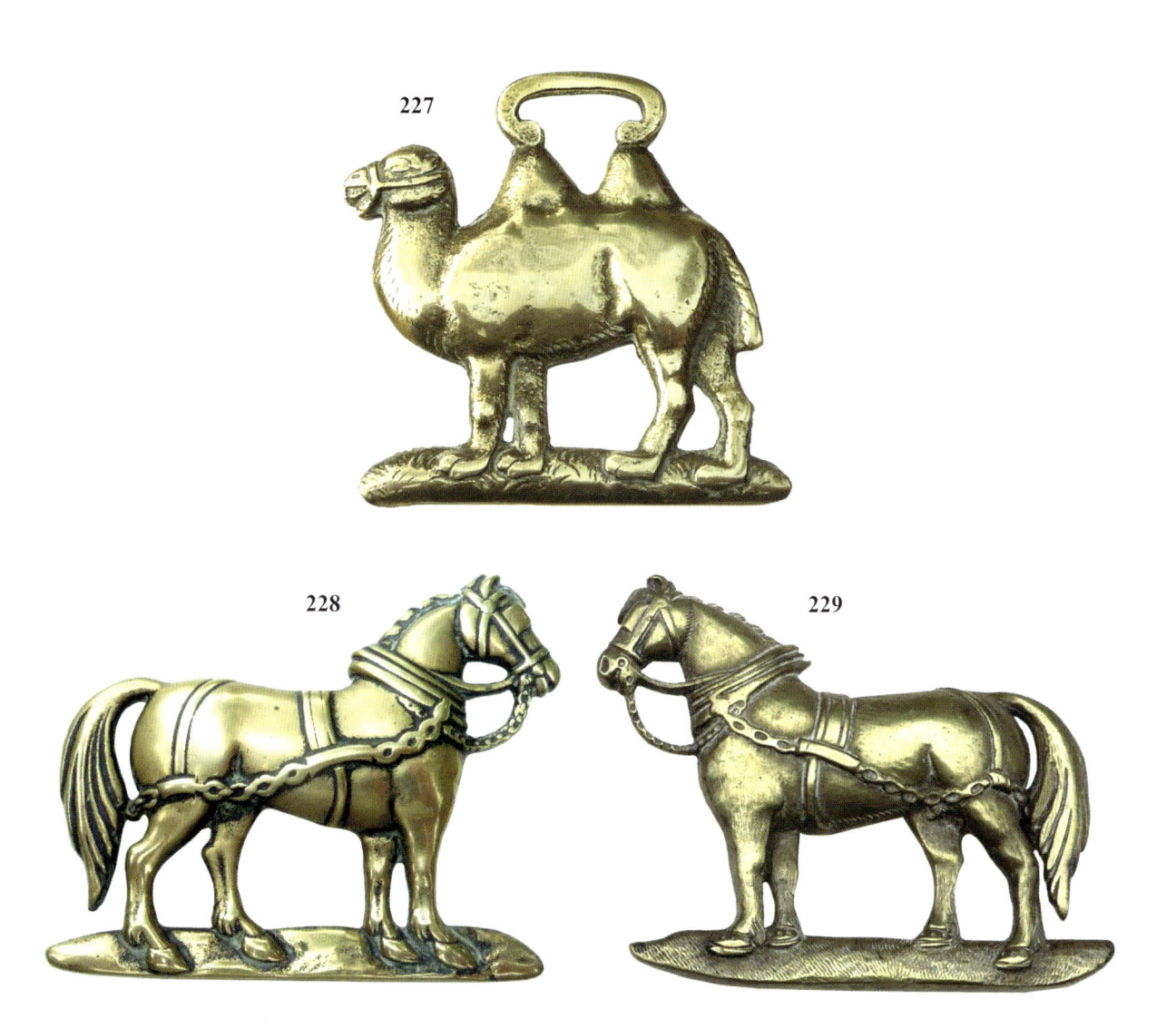

It is difficult to imagine a working horse in any of the traditional industries wearing some of the myriad animal brasses that were produced—unless of course the nature of the work were connected to the zoo or circus where the animals could be seen, in which case they would have served as advertisements. Perhaps this might explain why so few of these early examples are to be found.

**No. 227:** Bactrian camel, cast c.1900; excellent detail, very rare.
**No. 228:** 4-inch shanked stud, horse facing right; cast c.1875; fantastic detail, rare.
**No. 229:** hameplate with two iron loops, cast c.1875; detail even includes hoof nails!

[87]

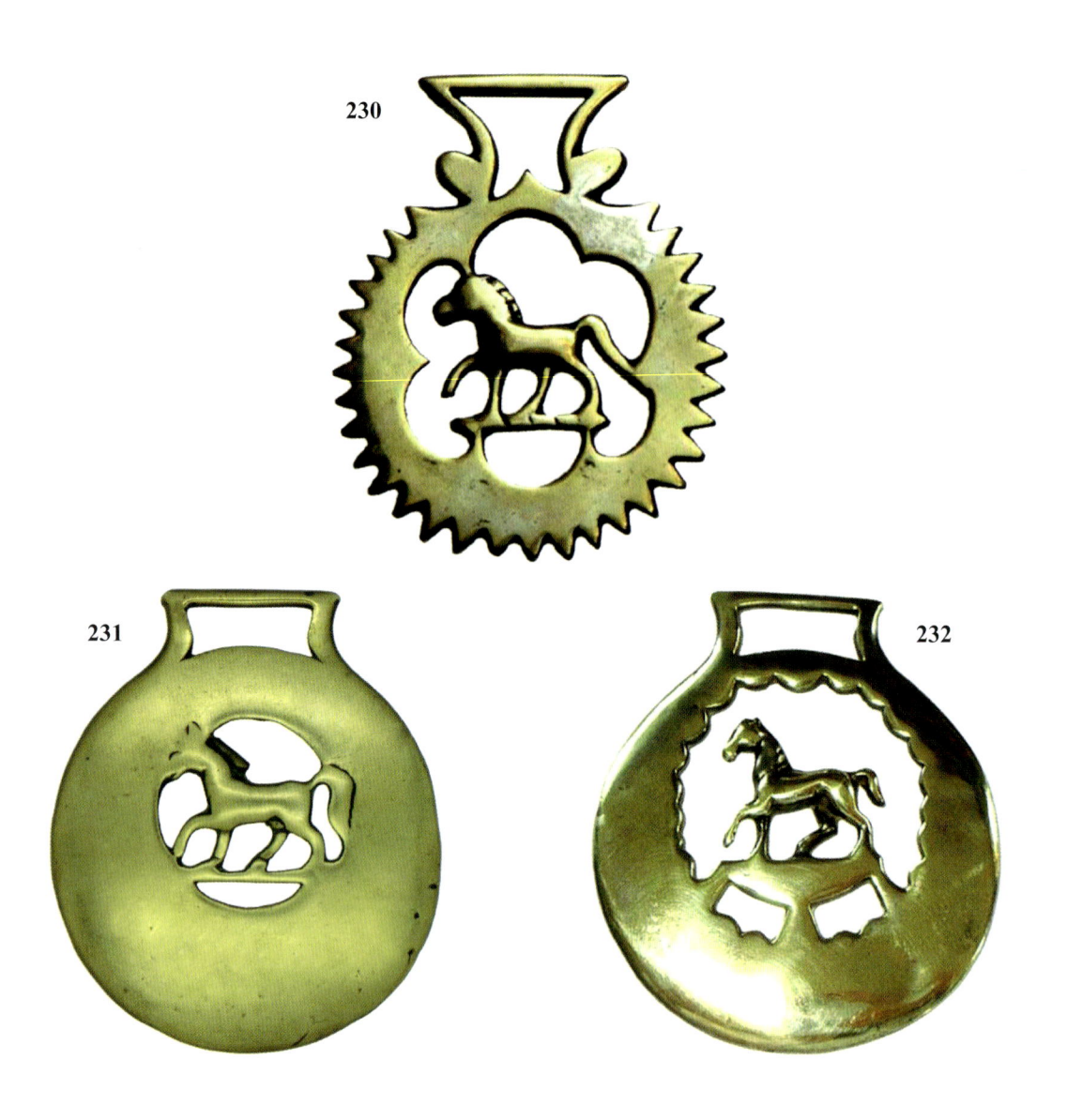

**No. 230:** the only known Sheffield Star type that featured a Horse Passant, probably dating c.1880-1885; this example has seen much wear and polish.
**No. 231:** previously unrecorded early brass, also much worn and polished.
**No. 232:** horse is double-sided and framed inside by cusped edge; unusual and rare.

**No. 233:** Lion Rampant with coronet on heraldic torque, a symbol of majesty and valour, unusually surrounded by a Sheffield Star frame; good detail, rare.
**No. 234:** Lion Passant Regardant in a wide-hanger crescent frame; seldom found.
**No. 235:** Lion Passant Guardant within a closed crescent; well-preserved detail.

**No. 236:** graceful curves of the frame sensitively complement those of the swan; superbly crafted brass, exceptional detail, well-preserved and rare, c.1880.

**No. 237:** classic 19th century example, notable for its simplicity and power. The applied Prancing Horse, lead-filled, traces its origin back to the 449 AD arrival in South East England of the legendary Hengist and Horsa brothers, plus their Anglo-Saxon army, who routed the Scots and Picts and founded the Kingdom of Kent. The White Horse Rampant (from the same family as its Prancing relative) was emblazoned on Horsa's battle flag and later adopted by Kent County as part of its official coat-of-arms.

# *Swingers*

**238**

The swinger, also known as a fly terret or fly head terret, was the sparkling jewel that crowned the harness. Today it is considered an icon of a bygone era and remains highly popular with collectors as an area of specialisation. Measuring 3 to 4 inches high, it was usually worn atop the bridle but might as well be seen mounted on the cart saddle or rump strap. There were hundreds of designs, many made to match specific facepieces, along with dozens of pre-1914 commemoratives. The great majority of swingers were produced with a circular frame, so much so that those with different shapes are comparatively rare. Example **No. 238**, shown here in full size because it is such an exceptionally large and unusual piece, was cast in the form of a clover leaf.

**No. 239:** flat Lyre frame with matching flat centre; Matthew Harvey catalogue, 1902.
**No. 240:** flat cross-Botonée centre, tightly fitted in rhombus-shape flat frame.
**No. 241:** flat clover leaf centre and matching frame (also known as "cottage loaf").

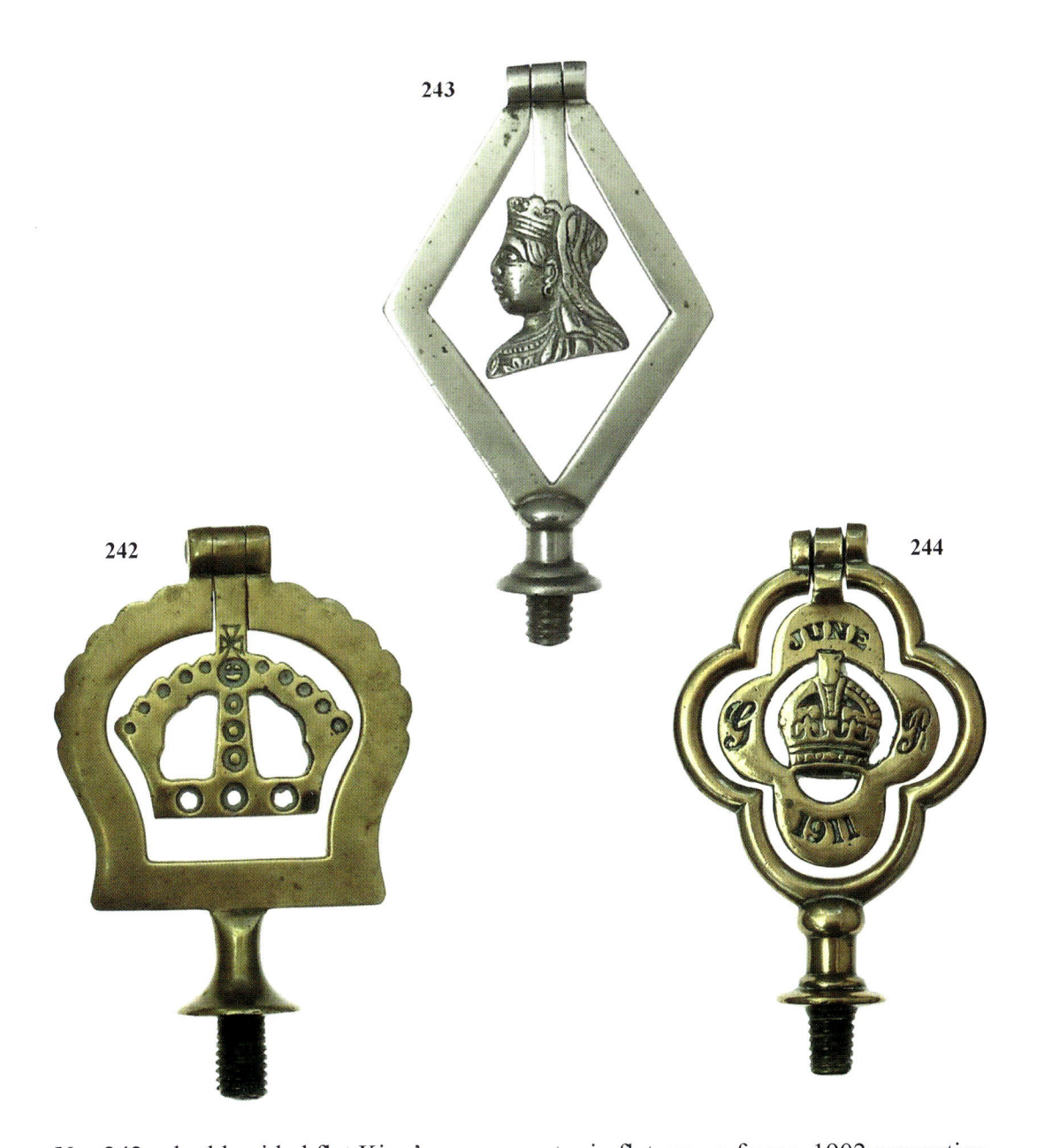

**No. 242:** double-sided flat King's crown centre in flat crown frame, 1902 coronation.
**No. 243:** white metal double-sided Victoria bust in flat diamond frame, 1897 Jubilee.
**No. 244:** double-sided centre in matching frame, 1911 coronation; R.E. Thacker Ltd.

**No. 245:** double-sided Queen's crown centre in round frame, 1887 Golden Jubilee.
**No. 246:** frame in shape of Victoria Cross; double-sided matching centre with cast young crowned head of monarch and legend "Queen Victoria – Empress of India – Born 1819 – Crowned 1838 – Married 1840 – Jubilee 1887".
**No. 247:** double-sided Jubilee Bust with Queen's mourning crown in flat frame, 1887.

[94]

**No. 248:** cast Maltese Cross centre in squared frame with scalloped corners.
**No. 249:** double-sided centre and flat frame; front with celluloid-protected portrait and "Edward VII – Crowned 1902"; reverse with crossed Union and patriotic flags and "Long Live The King"; Regd.354494, Wm. Overton Ltd.
**No. 250:** stamped double-sided centre in frame contoured to match, 1902 coronation.

[95]

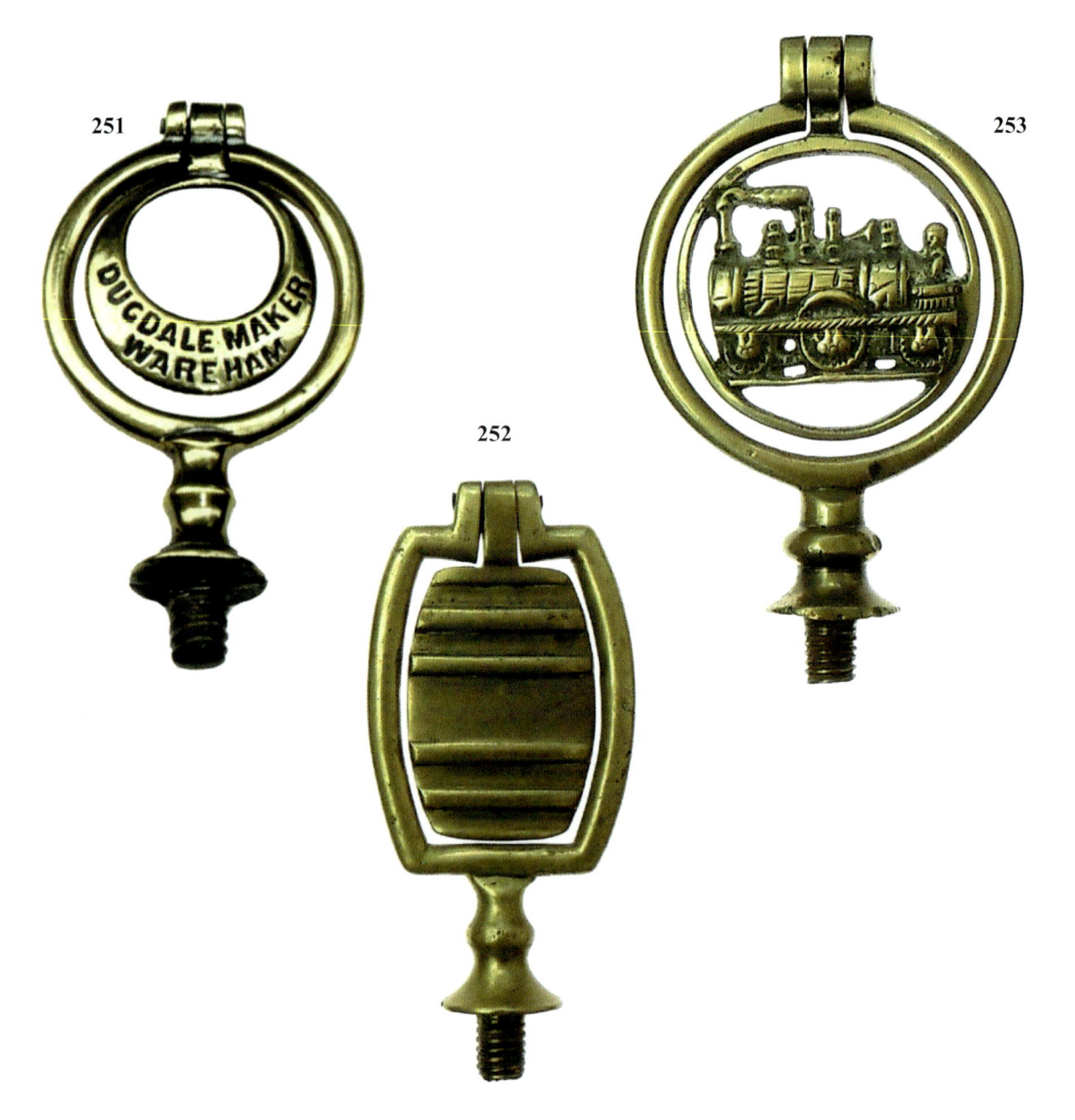

**No. 251:** Thos.B. Dugdale was a maker in Wareham, Dorset, 1879-1896; cast intaglio.
**No. 252:** double-sided barrel centre in matching frame; Thos. Crosbie catalogue, 1885.
**No. 253:** cast 2-2-2 wheel locomotive centre, superbly detailed, in round frame.

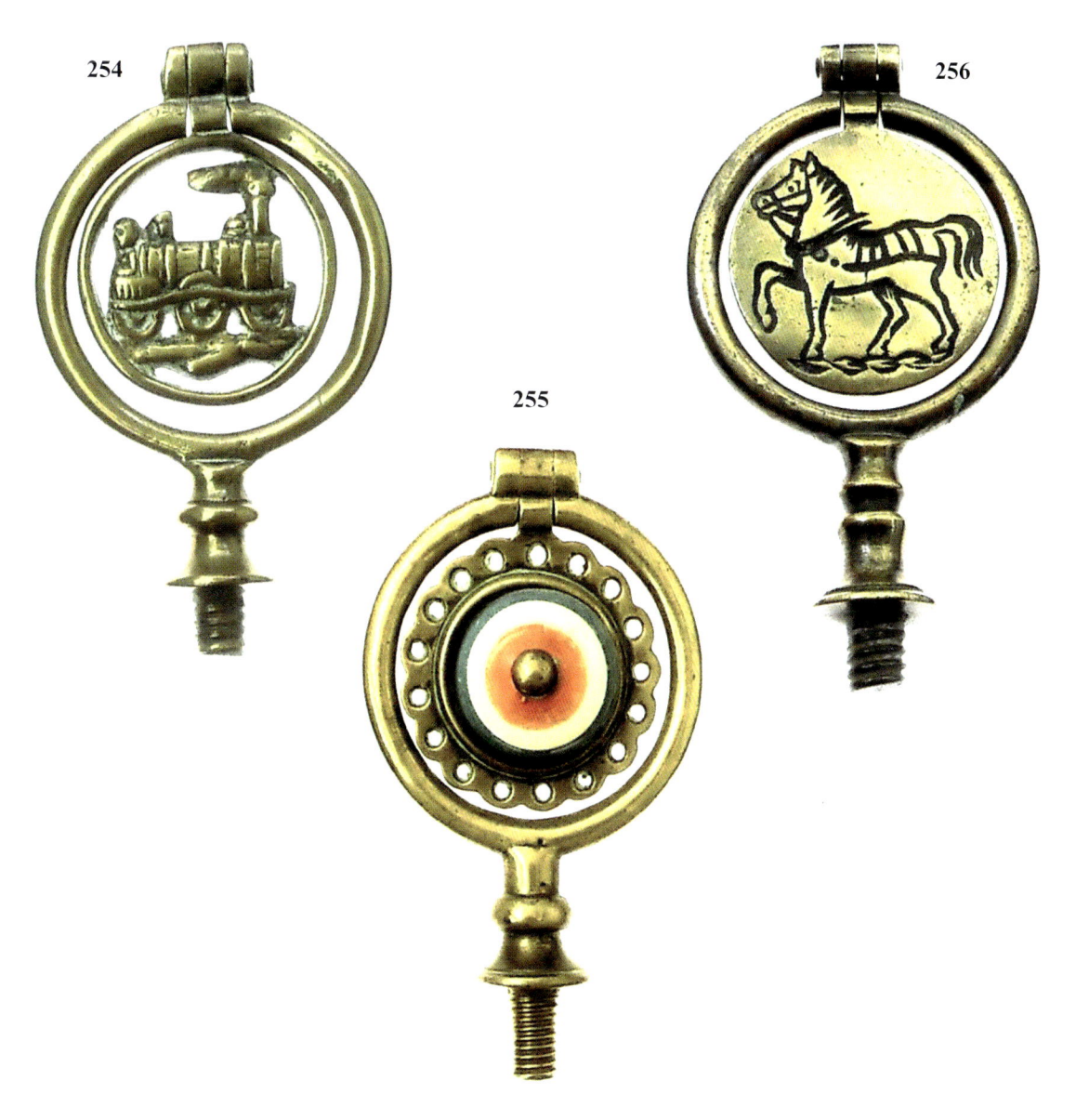

**No. 254:** cast 0-6-0 wheel locomotive centre in round frame; driver facing to the rear.
**No. 255:** patriotic Red White & Blue porcelain centre in round frame.
**No. 256:** disc centre with round frame; heavy horse in harness cast intaglio.

**No. 257:** cast anchor, meticulously detailed, in round frame.
**No. 258:** double-sided wheatsheaf in heraldic round frame, once in Malaher Collection.
**No. 259:** flat centre with cut-outs in matching frame; Thos. Crosbie catalogue, 1885.

[98]

**No. 260:** double-sided Staffordshire Knot in heart-shape frame; Thos. Crosbie, 1885.
**No. 261:** cast elephant centre in oval-shape frame; some detail lost due to polishing.
**No. 262:** cast "Lazy Carter" centre, sharply detailed, in flat frame with beveled edging.

# *Patterns & Oddities*

It has been said before—to touch and collect antique horse brasses is like holding history in your hands, like traveling back in time to rediscover the heritage of a bygone era. For many collectors the very essence of the hobby itself lies in such pursuit of history, the challenges of research and the pulsating excitement when answers are found. On a note of inspiration for the future, we therefore believe it fitting to end this second volume of the *Anthology* with a few examples that reflect the mysteries and delights still ahead for us all.

No. 263: cast intaglio for a saddler? coal merchant? contractor? haulier?; despite all the given specifics, this brass has defied research and is as yet unidentified.
No. 264: concentric circles in bas-relief around a flat centre boss, 19th century.
No. 265: right-handed, clockwise motion of the gammadion was ancient symbol for the revolving sun, the four levels of human existence and good luck.
No. 266: primitive early pattern with 20 perforations and uneven tooth edge.
No. 267: inverted Sheffield Star with applied boss and early "goal post" hanger.
No. 268: cast elongated heart features 53 perforated interstices, 19th century.
No. 269: ornate cast pattern formed by a ring of six stylised hearts, c.1885.
No. 270: three ogee curves mold this cast pattern, remarkable for its simplicity.

[100]

266 267 268 269 270

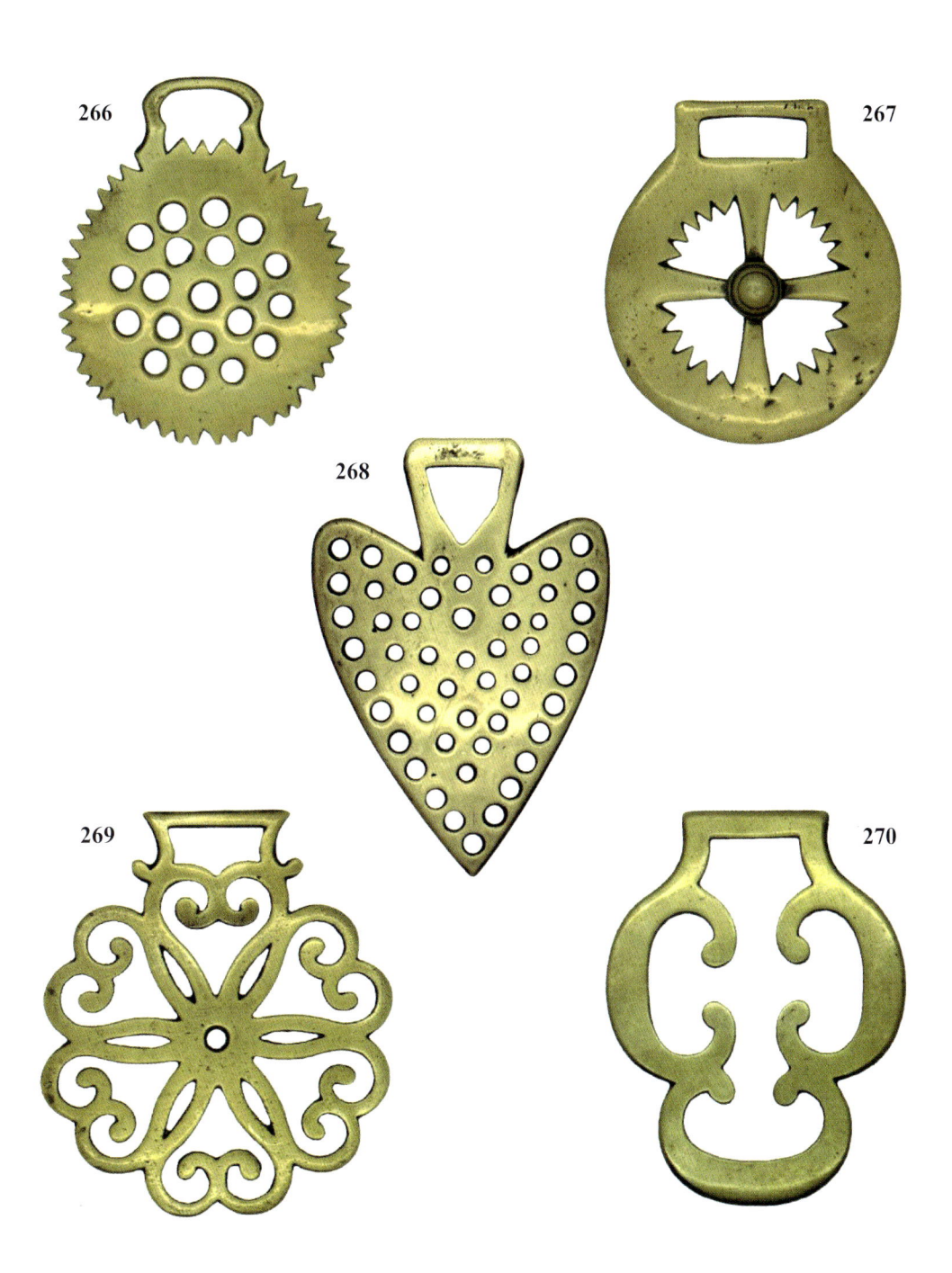

[101]

# Acknowledgements

On behalf of the Officers and Committee of the National Horse Brass Society, the authors would like to thank all those who so kindly contributed their time, indulgence and knowledge towards the publication of this second volume. It has been a rare privilege to access, record and use such a large number of superb brasses from so many of the finest collections in the world. Accordingly, we especially wish to recognise the following individuals:

Rolf Augustin, Stan Benton, Richard Booth, Allan Brewer, Ralph Chapman, Mrs. J. Clark, Gerald Dee, Franck and Esther Desjariges, John Dew, Joe Evans, the late Terry Keegan, the late Peter Lacey, Rankin Lewis, Peter Miller, Michael Mullens, Robert Prager, Mark Roberts, David Whetton and George Willett.

Our deepest gratitude goes, in particular, to Michael Ferguson for making available his extensive archives on saddlers, to Stephen Caunce for use of his photograph (opposite) and to Rolf Augustin for design, editing, formatting and production of the book.

We thank you sincerely, one and all!

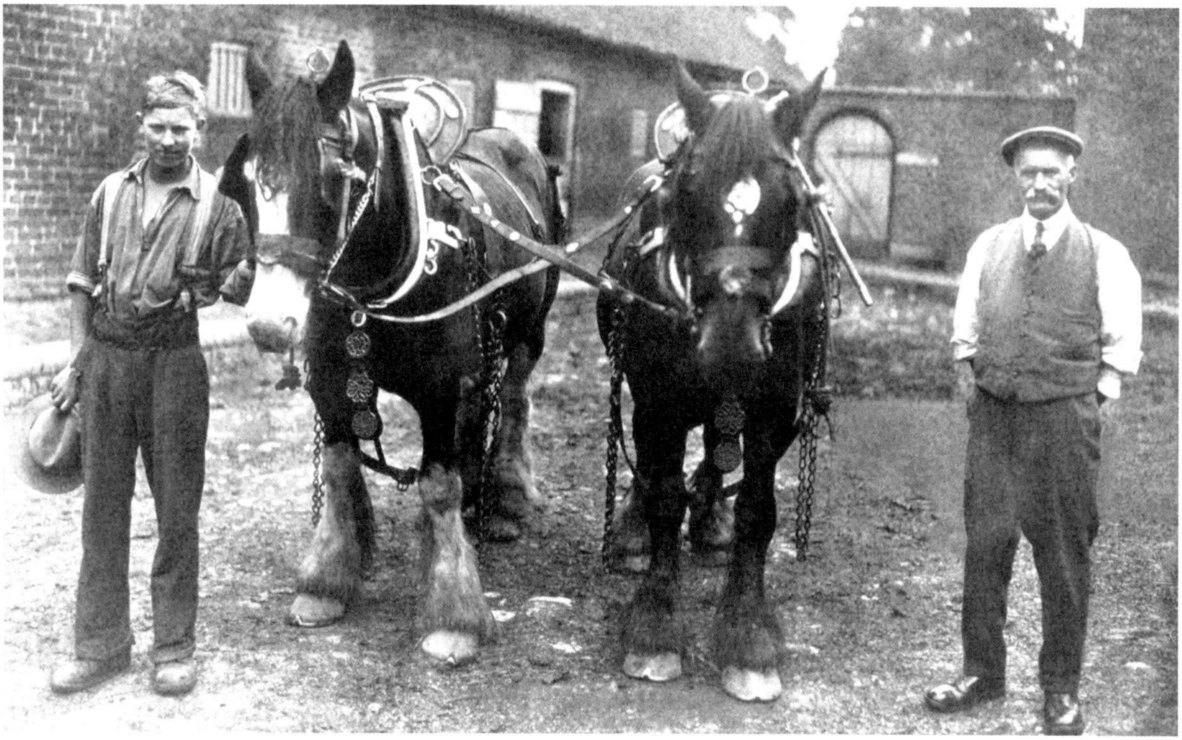

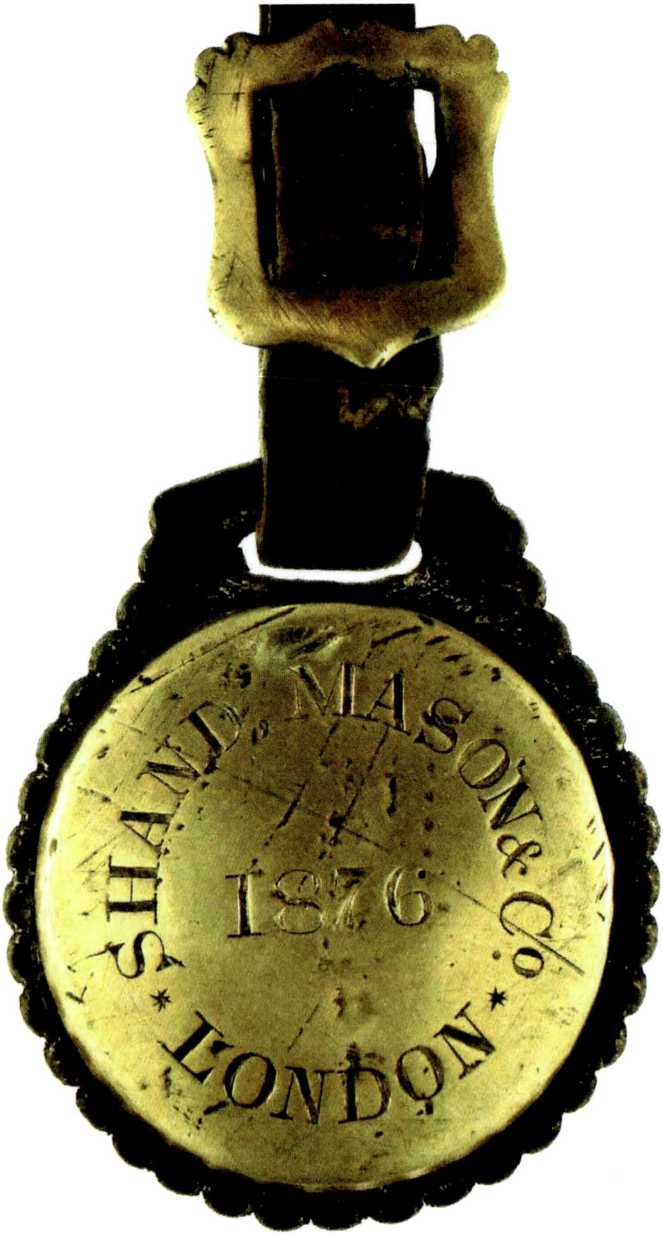
SHAND, MASON & Co
1876
LONDON

STAINES HORSE PARADE
Highly Commended
1904